The Write Spot
to Jumpstart Your Writing:
Discoveries

The Write Spot
to Jumpstart Your Writing

Discoveries

— Book 1 in The Write Spot Series —

Autumn 2017

Marlene Cullen, Editor

The Write Spot
to Jumpstart Your Writing:
Discoveries

© 2017 by Marlene Cullen

ISBN: 978-1-941066-25-6

Book design by Jo-Anne Rosen
Cover photo by Breana Marie
Jacuzzi Winery, Sonoma, CA

M. Cullen Enterprises
Petaluma, California
an imprint of Wordrunner Press

Dedicated to

writers and writing teachers,

the brave risk takers

Also Available in The Write Spot Series

The Write Spot to Jumpstart Your Writing: Connections
Writing from mothers and their children illustrate how we relate through stories.

"Heartfelt conviction, strong imagery, and the generational connections make the pieces in Marlene Cullen's *The Write Spot to Jumpstart Your Writing: Connections* an excellent anthology of mini-memoirs. The book is a powerful testament to the way the written word connects and inspires us. The prompts will help you write your own stories."

—B. Lynn Goodwin, WriterAdvice and author of
Never Too Late and *Talent*

The Write Spot: Reflections
A treasure chest of anecdotes, vignettes, and poems.

"To see the world in a grain of sand or the future in a ball of lightning, to see meanings in a psychedelic bubble or in a glass bottle of Coca-Cola, *Reflections* vividly mirrors elements of our multifaceted lives—imagined by a myriad of sharp-eyed writers. This anthology brings the everyday into focus with a brightness of spirit that we all can admire, and be inspired!"

—Kate F.

The Write Spot: Memories
Diverse narratives from fathers and their children embrace a common thread of love, disappointment, discoveries, and revelations.

"Marlene Cullen's collection of short essays compiled in *The Write Spot: Memories* unfolds like a gently-made, multicolored origami box. Each story is its own piece, its own regretful, loving, confusing, humorous, illuminating tale, yet held together by one theme that touches us all—our fathers and our memories of them when we were children, and our awakenings about them as we became adults. *Memories* is for anyone who has had a father whether present or absent, loving or distant, authoritarian or goofball. Authentic and relatable, each story is written with deep insight and love."

—Julie

The Write Spot: Possibilities
A mixture of playful, experimental, insightful stories as well as prompts and resources for writers.

"These words will touch your heart and might even move your pen."

—Brenda Bellinger, author of *Taking Root*

The Write Spot: Writing as a Path to Healing
Illustrates how to write about difficult topics without adding trauma.

"Quite possibly the most deeply moving volume in the Write Spot series. The contributing writers delve into the pain of their past, reveal their vulnerabilities, and share the lessons they've learned. Their courage is written on every page of this collection.

"Even while she's editing an anthology, Cullen has her mind on writers. She understands that writing through difficult life events can unearth strong emotions and memories and so she includes resources for the writer's mental and emotional support—and that's what makes the Write Spot series more than just a collection of stories."

—Elizabeth Beechwood

The Write Spot: Musings and Ravings from a Pandemic Year
Insightful writing reflecting emotions and experiences during a tumultuous year.

"What I appreciate most about *The Write Spot: Musings and Ravings from a Pandemic Year* is its cornucopia of honest exploration into the human condition during, but not exclusive to the COVID-era. Nature as nurturer is interwoven in this lively collection that is filled with wisdom, prompts, and inspiration for those seeking the lift of a literary life."

—Frances Rivetti

Contents

Lynn Levy

Cheryl Moore

Christine Renaudin

Su Shafer

Jo-Anne Rosen

Susan Bono

Marlene Cullen

Writing Resources

Introduction

I love freewrites ... writing freely, with no thoughts nor worries about the final product. I am fascinated with how the freewrite method of writing offers opportunities to explore and play with writing. You can be yourself (memoir/personal essay), you can be someone else (fiction), you can be a reporter (non-fiction/ essay).

My first experience with freewrites was with a gentle teacher who inspired writing by using creative prompts. My first time facilitating freewriting workshops was with friends in my parlor. We called our group "Wild Mindz," following the guidelines in Natalie Goldberg's book, *Writing Down the Bones*.

After two years of writing together, the Wild Mindz participants encouraged me to start a public writing group. Thinking about how prompts ignite ideas for writing, much like a spark, or a jumpstart for a vehicle, I decided to call this writing group, "Jumpstart." I've had the pleasure of writing with many Jumpstart writers these past twelve years, some of whose work appears in this anthology.

The writing in *Discoveries* originated with a word, a poem, or sometimes an object to inspire freewrites. This writing became polished pieces by writers who were willing to re-visit their original freewrites, tweak passages, and persevere with editing. As Pam Hiller, one of the participants in Jumpstart put it, "There is a vitality that sometimes appears in our freewrites. Reworking the piece can deepen the writing, living the theme of 'Discoveries.'"

At almost every writing event I attend, people mention how hard it is to find a supportive writing group.

Discoveries can be your personal writing group. If you join a writing group, perhaps you can use the prompts here or on The Write Spot Blog to inspire your writing: www.TheWriteSpot.us.

I hope *Discoveries* brings the joy of writing freely to you.

Marlene

Discoveries

An Exercise in Barbecuing

DS Briggs

Very recently I leapt into the world of backyard barbecuing. For years I have secretly wanted to learn to barbecue. In my family it was always my Dad's domain. However, I love grilled foods and got tired of waiting for Mr. Weber-Right to BBQ for me.

I proudly acquired a very big, shiny new Weber BBQ. It came with a grown-up sized grill width of twenty-two and a half inches. I dubbed my new friend "Big Boy."

Unfortunately, for me, Big Boy came in a big box with far too many pieces. It was with a definite leap of faith to undertake putting Big Boy together. He did not have written directions, nor a you-tube video and I have no degree in advanced "IKEA." Instead, Big Boy came with an inscrutable line drawing and lots of lines leading to alphabet letters. Still, I have my own Phillips's head screwdriver. I used to call it the star-thingie until an old boyfriend corrected me. But I digress. Suffice to say, after trials and even more errors, I constructed Big Boy.

Okay, so it took me three hours instead of twenty minutes, but Big Boy was upright and proud. I just wanted to admire my handiwork by this time and Big Boy was clean, so very clean. In fact, he was too clean to use. I postponed the baptismal fire and nuked my dinner that night.

In a couple of days, after repeated trips to the store for important and essential tools of the trade: A cover to keep Big Boy dry and clean, real mesquite wood to feed him, and long-handled tongs. For my own protection I bought massive mittens. I was almost ready to launch Big Boy. A few forays into the garage for additional must haves—my landlord's trusty but rusty charcoal chimney fire starter can with a grate on the bottom and handle on the side and a dusty, spidery partial bag of charcoal in case my mesquite wood failed to turn into coals. I was finally ready to light up the barbecue.

I chose to inaugurate Big Boy on a humid, somewhat breezy day. No gale force winds were predicted. As a precaution, I hosed down the backyard weeds. I found matches from the previous century and a full Sunday paper for starter fuel. The directions to stuff the bottom of the charcoal chimney can with crumpled newspaper and then load up the top part with either charcoal or wood sounded easy enough. I chose to use the mesquite wood based on advice from Barbecue Bob, a friend of mine.

I lit the chimney and soon had enough white smoke to elect the Pope. I waited the prerequisite twenty minutes for coals to appear. Nada. Nope. No coals in sight. The wood had not caught fire, although the paper left a nice white ash.

Hungry, but not deterred, I re-stuffed the bottom of the charcoal chimney with more newspaper and set the whole chimney on top of a mini-Mount St. Helens pile of newspaper. I found smaller bits of wood since the lumber did not ignite. I lit the new batch of newspapers again.

After a second dose of copious white smoke, miracle of miracles, the splinters of wood caught fire. Finally, it produced enough smoke for the oleanders to start talking.

"You do know it is a red flag day." I know bushes don't really talk, so I assumed the warning came from the owner of the fish-belly-white legs and flip-flops standing behind the tall, overgrown oleanders.

Having no clue what Flip-Flops meant, I explained that I was trying to learn how to BBQ. I asked what she meant by red flag day and she said that it was extreme fire danger in the hills. Aside from the fact that there was not a hill in sight, I told her that I had the hose at ready. I also asked Flip if BBQing was banned on red flag days. She didn't know, however, I think I heard the word fire bug. Perhaps she just wanted to let me know that she knew who was playing with matches on a red flag day in case the fire department asked.

Reassuring Neighbor Fire Watch, I carefully emptied the chimney's coals onto Big Boy's smaller, lower but still sparkling clean grill. Using my mitts, I gently crowned Big Boy with the very clean, shiny huge upper grill. The sacrificial chicken had, at last, a final resting place.

Whoosh! The previously white Pope smoke was now black and voluminous. Turns out olive oil makes lots of good smoke and less-than-helpful flare ups of flame. With my hands still ensconced in bright red mittens and using a very long tong, I turned the chicken. Only slightly blackened. I kept turning the chicken every five or ten minutes. More black, but not at the briquet stage—yet.

I figured I had better recheck my BBQ Bible, the thick one with pictures so you can compare your results with theirs. Their advice was to cook the chicken until it had an internal temperature of 189 degrees Fahrenheit. I hoped Fire Watch was not watching because I dangerously left my BBQ unattended to go rummage through my kitchen drawers in search of an instant read thermometer. I knew that I would need it someday when I bought it a decade earlier. I inserted it and watched it slowly rise to 145 degrees. Only 44 more degrees to go but I was starving and the coals were cooling! I knew this because according to said Bible you hold your hand above the coals and count three Mississippi's for good heat. By the time I had counted "One Mississippi, two Mississippi, three Mississippi ... fifteen Mississippi," even I could tell the coals were dead. I pulled the chicken off the grill. The skin was definitely done. Delicious? No. Blackened? Yes. Delectable? No. Vaguely resemble the BBQ Bible's picture? Not at all.

So for the lesson summary: Two hours of perseverance resulting in one hardly edible, even when finished-in-the-oven chicken. Adding insult to injury I had a very dirty, sticky, greasy, too-large-for-my-sink grill to scrub.

Lesson learned: find a home for Big Boy and call take-out.

Prompt: Write about a leap you have taken.

Hair Encounters of the Cursed Kind

DS Briggs

Mom and I had a running battle about my hair. At seven years old, all I wanted was a pony tail or even two pony tails, one above each ear. All Mom wanted was an easy-to-maintain pixie cut that was accomplished by putting a bowl on my head and chopping away. Since she was bigger and more powerful than me and could brush hair harder than any soul on earth … she won the hair battle.

My luck changed, or so I thought, when I was allowed to grow my hair longer than two inches. I did not know what fiendish plan Mom had cooked up for me.

The sneak attack came quite swiftly after chores were done one Saturday.

A Toni attacked me. Yes, my very own home permanent. This Toni person must have hated kids to allow this wretched procedure in her name.

Swathed in an oversized towel and bent backwards over the kitchen sink, the first step to be endured was the shampoo, followed by yank-the-hair into countless sections. Using a pink rattail comb, my hair was divided into matchbook-sized hanks. Each hank was wrapped with a teensy square of tissue paper. With another firm tug Mom rolled each hank around a pink, pointy-spine curler. After a final firm yank she snapped the hinge of the spiny curler. Soon my whole suffering scalp was gouged by rows of pink curlers.

The second step in this maniacal process began with Mom mixing the patented Toni solution and pouring it into their trademarked squeeze bottle. We placed a towel over my mouth and nose. I made sure to scrunch the towel over my eyes to keep them from getting burned. Mom took a cotton ball and saturated each damn curler with the acidic nose-clearing eye-watering ammonia based perm solution. When she was satisfied she had drowned the curlers, the kitchen timer was set for exactly twenty-five minutes.

After a very long twenty-five minutes the third wretched step began as she would bend me back over the sink to rinse and yank the curlers out. Another rinse followed with a vigorous dry and unfurling curls.

VOILA! Instant transformation from girl to poodle. I had enough curls to make me wish I had my pixie back.

Sure evidence of Mom's reverse psychology. Again.

Prompt: A childhood memory

Laguna Light

DS Briggs

Leaves fall softly to the ground.
The mown hay piles look dormant.
Tiny acorns thud to earth
And the whole sky quiets.

Soft steam arises from the creek,
Crawdads bundle their mud balls.
Spiders wait for their webs to dry.
As the morning light awakes the sky.

Catching the wind, the lace ball of seeds sway;
In contrast to the crickets hopping, leaping,
Joyfully living, at least for a while, among the
Brown and fallen grasses.

Life in the laguna continues.
On its path of interconnected individuals,
Living and dying in the moment, we
Are reminded of our guest status.

*Inspired by the poem "Our Lives Pass Away"
by David Budbill*

Missed Opportunities

DS Briggs

I was deprived of brown bagged school lunches. I never had a lunch box with a sandwich wrapped in wax paper. Never got to eat or trade sandwiches made with squishy white balloon bread. Missed out on dried-out baloney, peanut butter and grape jelly or tuna fish saturated bread. I missed out on homemade cookies, Hostess cupcakes, and Twinkies. I never got to carry a Nancy Drew or Dale Evans thermos. Worst of all my best and second best friends were cold lunch people.

I missed out on all the wonders of bagged lunches because my mom was convinced that buying a hot lunch was more cost effective. I have often wondered if the fact that she did not like to cook or grocery shop factored into her decision.

In the early 1960's at Charles Wright Elementary School the janitor was in charge of setting up the lunch room. Mr. Gino supervised his rowdy sixth grade boys as they pulled the benches and tables from their hiding place under the stage and set them in rows. Since students were assigned tables by class and whether they were eating hot lunch or cold lunch, hot lunch tables were near the kitchen, cold lunch near the exits. In the days before air conditioned schools, this could be an advantage or disadvantage.

Hot lunchers carried meal tickets with the days of the week printed on yellow card stock. After it was hole-punched we picked up a green or tan melamine tray with little square and rectangle spaces. I liked the divided sections because the canned fruit and vegetables stayed separated from each other and everything else. We slid our trays onto the metal counter that fronted the hair-netted and white-aproned cafeteria ladies armed with their stainless steel ladles. No sneeze guards in those days so we had a chance to tell them about our new dog or bike.

The kitchen moms ladled whatever was on the menu. We usually had a scoop of fruit cocktail. If you were really, really lucky you got a bright red maraschino cherry piece. The canned peaches and applesauce were not as exciting. Next in the line of anticipation came a vegetable. Scooped mashed potatoes or canned corn on a good day, lima beans or creamed corn on a not-so-good day.

As we pushed our trays down the counter, we waited to see what might be plopped in the largest rectangle— on great days, a hamburger or chili while on not-so-great days— mystery-meat or an equally unidentifiable casserole. On Fridays though, whether you were Catholic or not, fish sticks were tonged into the slot. Milk cartons plucked from a metal basket filled out the tray. Walking with extreme care, to keep our food in its assigned slot, we made our way to our table.

We could see the cold lunch kids swapping and sigh. No one traded anything on the hot lunch side. I am sure the cold lunchers became stock traders or negotiators. Cost effective or not, I think I missed some career training opportunities. Thanks, Mom.

Prompt: School Lunches

DS Briggs

DS Briggs is a retired school teacher. She taught students with visual impairments for over 30 years. Now she is a devoted dog owner and revels in the freedom of retirement with plenty of time to walk her dog. Besides writing, DS loves to read and dreams of seeing all of the National Parks in an RV. She and her dog reside in Santa Rosa, California.

Words of Encouragement:

1. Your thoughts may flow more easily if you are writing with a comfortable pen and paper that feels good under your pen.
2. Learning to listen to conversations around you is helpful when trying to recreate dialogue or gather new ideas.
3. Shutting out your internal critic vastly improves the whole process.
4. When sharing your work, chose an audience who have no agenda to make themselves feel better at your expense.

Amour

Karen Ely

He pulled her tightly against his chest, struggling to forge an invisible connection between his heart and hers. She was so beautiful with auburn hair and snapping brown eyes. Her cheeks flushed fetchingly, and her lips were ripe, a luscious red. She smelled of powder, lavender talc, and her breath hinted wintergreen and promise.

He held her tiny hand tightly in his fist. There was substance to it, a tender strength, and he smiled slightly, picturing the dimples he knew rested under the base of each milky white finger. His hand cupped her warm, supple waist. He tingled as he felt her corset beneath the silk, holding her in, holding her back. As he drew her towards him, he cocked his head and pushed his face into hers.

"Look at me" he commanded with silent, burning intensity. She turned her face away, eyes half lidded, expression wistful. He exhaled softly, and she felt his breath fan across her cheek. She murmured, and he leaned in, the red stubble of his ginger beard mere inches from her upturned nose. "What was that, Cherie?" the question rumbled from his chest, aching and raspy, "Tell me, mon amour."

The music faded and the clinking of glasses and boisterous laughter all blended together in a comfortable buzz. Long lashes fluttering like butterflies, she sighed softly, "Your breath is terrible. You need a mint."

Prompt: Inspired by Renoir's "Dancing at Bougival"

Baby Girl

Karen Ely

I borrowed a star from the infinite sky. I planted it under my heart, absorbing it into my being. I fed it with love and it filled me with wonder. It flowed through my veins and shot from my fingertips into an imperfect world.

I tried to close my hands around it, hold it in my palms and bind it to me. But to truly love, there is no grasping, no expectation. So I uncurled my fingers, unclenched my fist, loved with an honest, open hand. One pulsating, twinkling beam until the next.

My heart splintered when my star returned to the night sky. Too soon ... forever too soon. All in this world is borrowed; no promise of time, no guarantee of more than this one, precious moment ... but even on a dark, moonless night, I can look up and know that my star is there. She waits in that eternity for me.

Prompt: Something borrowed

Barbara's Braid

Karen Ely

Weaving strands of amber honey
Over, under, around and through
Silky locks of shimmer sunlight
Plaited patterns, three by two

Over, under, around, and through
Brush strokes cultivate the threads
Plaited patterns three by two
A tapestry of golds and reds

Brush strokes cultivate the threads
Silky locks of shimmer sunlight
Plaited patterns, three by two
Weaving strands of amber honey

Prompt: Write a pantoum.

Disguised Blessing

Karen Ely

It is ugly and jagged and cuts me in half. A permanent zipper down the middle of my chest. A scar that doesn't tan like the rest of my skin, vertically dividing my torso and evoking questions and comments whenever I dare a low-cut neckline. I wear it like a badge of honor, like a war medal that I earned in battle. It is a testament to my spirit, and a sign of kinship that I share with a most precious person from my past.

My baby girl had a scar just like this one. My sweet Caroline, who had open-heart surgery four days after she was born. She was diagnosed hours after she came hurtling into the world, and spent the rest of her short life fighting to survive. She defied logic, and stayed with me much longer than any doctor predicted. She had the heart of a lion.

Losing her shattered me. The pain in my heart was a physical thing, visible in the dullness of my eyes and the droop of my defeated shoulders. I pressed on with life; I had to. My other daughter deserved a real mother. She needed me. I moved past the pain, into a numbness of soul, not dead but not truly alive either. I pushed myself harder, and exhausted myself struggling to do the right things.

Six years after Caroline died, I was given a physical, tangible explanation for my fatigue: I also had a congenital heart defect. Not as severe as my daughter's, the hole in my heart had hidden undetected for 34 years. The odd flipping and flopping that I felt was not my imagination, it was my heart, dangerously enlarged, trying inefficiently to power my being. I jokingly told my cardiologist, who had been Caroline's doctor as well, that I'd been right all along. My heart truly was broken.

I had it repaired, and oddly, the experience helped to heal my soul. I was gifted with the opportunity to see, feel, and taste what my daughter had endured. I was able to understand, as much as anyone can, what a life of surgery and hospitals would have been for my sweet Caroline. I also came to realize that I WANTED to be here. I wanted to live and love and survive with the family I have here on earth.

My scar reminds me that I am here because I choose to be. It is loud and glaring and defiant. It says that I am strong and I am a fighter. My troubled heart turned out to be a blessing in disguise —something bad that turned into something good—linking me to a special little soul I hold most dear.

Prompt: Something bad that turned out good

When Prayers Happen

Karen Ely

It usually happens in the moments in-between. After those breaths inward, where time is suspended between thought and action; between seeing and saying.

It can happen at scenic vistas, where the sun is climbing the Saguaro-pocked mountains, spilling molten gold through the sagebrush and shining on the flinty shards of granite that carpet the wash.

It can happen in front of the bathroom mirror, sleepers still in my eyes, hair wild and uncombed. As the minty gel of the new tube of toothpaste effortlessly uncurls onto the wet bristles of my toothbrush.

It can happen at any beach, in that instant before I reach up to pull back wisps of hair that have blown into my eyes. The wave has already rumbled to the shore, and silver foam is in a lather. On the sand, bubbles magically erupt on the surface.

It can happen as I run my fingers up and down my sleeping dog's spine, gently massaging her brittle bones. My hand sinking into the cotton candy fluff of her summer coat, and absorbing the warmth of her dog-soul as it silently purrs in gratitude.

This is when prayers happen, in those in-between moments when I'm filled with silent wonder and awe and contentment at the way things are. Time freezes, and I worship in the church of my life.

Prompt: What inspires you?

Karen Ely

There are some who swear that Karen Ely was born with her nose firmly planted in a book. She is a life-long, voracious reader with an insatiable appetite for unusual words, lilting phrases, and absurd stories. Repurposing her endless collection of literary consumption into new, "wordly" compositions seems only natural for Karen. Reading is inhaling and writing is exhaling. After spending her first 25 years dreaming of escape from the small town she grew up in, and the next 25 desperately trying to get back, Karen is finally at home in the San Francisco Bay Area. She delights in difficult crossword puzzles, humorous obituaries, and anything baked by her husband James.

Words of Encouragement

I used to think that to be a writer you needed a "big story" to tell, or some epic wisdom to impart.... and I, being me, never felt that I had anything truly compelling to say. I've been writing almost since I could read, but I never shared my work. I never really thought I was a "writer."

All of that changed when I started Jumpstart. In a safe, encouraging environment I was able to open myself and my writing, and what I found was that we ALL have stories and a unique view point to share. We can all be writers.

A funny thing happened when I started writing and sharing. I began to understand myself. Amidst the descriptive words and linear plot lines, forgotten truths and buried revelations made many things clearer to me. So not only was I writing for the sheer joy of making art with words, I was also writing as a way to reevaluate my point of view, to reimagine realities.

There are millions of reasons to write — as many reasons as there are individuals inhabiting the planet. It is all valid.

It is all valuable. You can write to communicate with others, or write just to communicate with yourself. Open your mind and let yourself flow out, onto the written page. It feels good, and you may even surprise yourself.

Feminine is Fabulous

Pam Hiller

Girls have the best
never think to rest
on the laurels
that make quarrels

with men who work
they offer perks
so they can rest
in little nests.

They never cry
or wonder why
the world is such,
it is too much

for fragile brains
to take the strains
they need to rest
to have the best.

*Prompt: Poem Sketching, a free-write exercise by
the late poet Sanford Lyne*

Journey

Pam Hiller

The first leg of our trip to Nashville began with a Thursday afternoon flight. As Jon spent the three hours attending to job details on his laptop, I found myself increasingly staring at cloudscapes from my window seat. Snow covered mountaintops appeared to float on a sea of white clouds. Sunset over New Mexico's red rock formations astounded with light, shadows, reflections, as earth and sky interacted. Dusk's purple light soothed west Texas plains where vein-like rivers flowed. The night sky, increasing lightning flashes on the horizon, thrilled as our plane was diverted from Dallas to Wichita Falls.

A question began emerging in my mind and heart. I felt myself a part of the grandeur, the immense mystery I was observing. On the other hand, it was apparent that an individual life is literally invisible in nature's vast scale. Does a single human existence really matter?

Saturday afternoon we attended a ceremony naming our former high school auditorium after a beloved drama teacher. City officials presented a declaration from the mayor declaring it Kent Cathcart Day in Nashville. Two former pupils gave speeches describing this man's profound impact in teaching students to dare living authentically. Approximately half of the people in the audience were students from his first theater class in 1972 through his last class in 1999.

Once the speeches ended Kent sat in a brown leather armchair on the stage, a fatherly figure sharing his thoughts and observations. Amid the laughter and memories he expressed a few simple statements about his faith, in a way as a public school teacher he hadn't before. He told us that every morning before teaching he would attend an early morning mass. He spoke of allowing one's active life to lead to a place of silence where God could be heard. He emphasized that whatever spiritual path one followed making room for this silent space was an essential component. As in our youth, we listened spell-bound.

Post celebration several former classmates met at a nearby home. We talked late into the night describing adventures (and misadventures) connected to time we spent in our home away from home, classroom S-01. As the evening progressed it became apparent that each of us had felt seen, attended to by Kent, in ways that deeply affected us both as teenagers and adults.

So, to return to my question—does a single human life matter? What I experienced that weekend is that each life radiates outward in circles we can't possibly imagine. While I still felt awed by the unknowable mystery of it all, I also felt more grounded in the feeling that the integrity of each person's actions is important. We all contribute to the world in ways that are obvious, and in ways we may never know.

Prompt: Notes from writing journal

Lessons

Pam Hiller

The poet William Stafford said, "The place we meet the muse is in our own true voice." After years when I struggled to do only the right things and to be perfect, searching to find authentic words and actions has become an entirely new journey.

From the beginning of first grade I was taught there is a right and a wrong way to think. All responses can be precisely measured as correct or, heaven forbid, incorrect. Increasingly I found myself out of sync with this program by becoming too interested in assigned tasks—either dreaming of colorful possibilities or following promising investigations in search of answers to problems. Either way it led to one more demerit on a report card in the *Starts and completes work on time* column.

Little by little this approach to education became training in subtraction—subtracting rich dreams, closing openness to new experiences, reining in experimentation. Success equaled accumulating reams of information; sorting through endless piles of facts like a miser with his gold, separating from love of learning about life while building ivory towers of abstractions.

A young person needs both guidance and experience. Some knowledge can only be deeply taught person-to-person. When a wise teacher offers direction from his or her storehouse of experiences it illuminates the dark places where a student's knowledge and ability have not yet taken root.

During my apprenticeship with an oriental rug restorer in my early twenties, antique carpets with complex damages were presented to me to repair. Given minimal training in necessary techniques, I was then left to find my way. Aziz, my restoration teacher, gave simple instructions, "Do not take out mistakes. Too much worrying blocks you from finding what is needed. Find a way to make whatever progress you have made work. When you have made 10,000 mistakes, then you will be a master."

As I wrangled my way through knotted threads, I panicked. As I wrestled with wrong choices, I cursed Aziz. When he offered a hint of advice to smooth the way, I began to see this was the best way to learn. He was teaching me how to think—to slow down in front of uncertainty, to study what was in front of me, to figure things out.

I have often returned to this practical training in facing life challenges. Honest questions can lead to the next step, which opens to the next, and so on. Answers are not prefabricated programs pasted onto a messy human being. Faith and effort are involved. Carefully paying attention to hunches, facts, and training allows experiences of connection to appear—moments of hearing my true voice, honestly filling my place in this world. Inspiration comes not from finding a perfect life, but in exploring ways to meet and love the life I find.

Prompt: Speak your truth

Slow Arrival

Pam Hiller

The birds are courting at Shollenberger Park.
Each male red-winged blackbird sits
On cattail stalk proclaiming, "Look at me,
I am the best. Gaze upon my magnificence."
The female bird yawns, she's seen it all before.

Young men, drunk on testosterone, swagger
In the parking lot. The next generation
Who knows everything, shouting immortality
From mud spattered pickup trucks.

Tempering seasons pass.

Old man walking the wetlands path.
Back not as straight, but heart more open.
Listening to song of the sun, ballad of the moon.
Gnarly shells of experience protecting
Hard won wisdom pearls.

Prompt: Inspired by the poem "New Year" by Mary Sarton

True Worth

Pam Hiller

As I walked into Kmart recently, a familiar feeling came over me. I felt so at home, so able to drop pretenses. Even the smells brought memories of another time, a place, where the dignity of a human being wasn't solely measured by the dollars in his paycheck.

I never realized we were poor.

My father's two jobs as a printer, fulltime swing shifts at Rand McNally and twice weekly day shifts at the Nashville Banner newspaper, made it possible for Mom to stay home with my sister and me. His work left him tired, with ink under his nails and in the creases of weathered hands, but swing shifts, 4 p.m. until midnight, often allowed precious hours together during the daytime. On hot summer mornings, before work, he would often take us to nearby Pine Springs Resort, a small lake set in the trees, with a tiny real sand beach. Dad taught us girls dog paddling by catching us as we splashed around in the shallows while minnows brushed against our bare legs. When Dad thought I was ready, he stayed right beside me, stroke by stroke, as I learned to swim in deep water to the wooden raft floating at the lake's center.

I never realized we were poor.

Once a year we shopped for school clothes at Sears. Mom would say, "If you choose simple clothes, they won't look cheap," my first lessons in discerning quality. Afterwards, a short drive south took us past Dixie Used Cars, 2nd Chance Bail Bonding, and under a rusting railroad bridge to our next destination, Cumberland Footwear. In the dark, musty, shoe outlet we were allowed to buy a pair of sneakers and a pair of school shoes. This extravagant day came with instructions that the new clothes were "never to be worn for play, only school." I floated home like a princess with my treasures.

I never realized we were poor.

While Dad was at work Mom took us to the public library. The first stop, find the newest issue of Highlights magazine. Sitting on child size chairs Patty, Mom, and I would search for every object in the hidden picture puzzle. Afterwards, each of us would check out an armload of books, with Mom borrowing classical music records for good measure. At home Mom read aloud poetry, *Black Beauty, Little Women*. We pored over art books while Beethoven played on the stereo.

I never realized we were poor.

When late autumn arrived Dad would take on seasonal employment, working his usual evenings off as a sales clerk at Spartans Department Store, the Kmart before there was a Kmart. Years later my mother told me that, while laughing like children, she and Dad would use his employee's discount, fill a shopping cart with toys and clothes, and put them on the lay-away plan. Early Christmas day my parents' eyes glowed as brightly as Santa's while they watched my sister and I rejoice in the magical morning.

Because richness filled our lives, I never realized we were poor.

Prompt: Inspired by the poem "The Perfect Mother" by Maria Mazziotti Gillan

Pam Hiller

Pam draws upon the storytelling traditions of her Tennessee childhood as inspiration for her writing. She has been blessed with a mother, relatives, and friends who know how to tell a good tale. Book-filled libraries have provided her with endless sources of wonder and interesting thoughts to ponder. It is Pam's wish to write from the heart, from life experiences that influence her changing sense of being alive.

Words of Encouragement

One of the joys of the Jumpstart program has been to join with others in sharing writings before they are polished, when still close to the source. While each piece can be developed more fully, they are valuable as-is. Free writes offer unique opportunities for communal storytelling. Like rustic pieces of Japanese pottery or vibrant tribal weavings, they have the power to touch essential human feelings.

all unsaid

Alex Inaudi

all unsaid

breathes fire into shrouds
sewn almost shut

ungrounds a puny cage
roofless and slight

blows some cloudy vagrant
out beyond lost

clutches at hopes for this
tongue crashing free

Prompt: Silence

ambition's poison

Alex Inaudi

ambition's poison

work in secret
to perfect skill

bury gems in
mountainous drafts

let time's sandblast
buff slag to gleam

and pray neglect
leach all but truth

burn pale but fierce
that future scorch

Prompt: Yearning: A self-interview

Face Time

Alex Inaudi

"Smiling more," Crowsfeet said, "can give a lovely crinkle."

"Here we go," moaned Forehead. "Again with the wrinkle advice."

"That's not what—" Crowsfeet began.

"Wrinkle's what you mean!" Forehead snapped.

Throat cleared itself. "Easy, Fore. Crow's got a point."

Forehead reddened, as Throat continued, "How 'bout you, Eyes, you like smiling?"

Eyes looked bashfully down. Blushing, Cheek nudged gently, "Sure brings out your sparkle."

Eyes widened a moment then blinked, as Lips turned up. "Guess you're outnumbered, Fore."

Beads of sweat broke out there, while the rest of the face just … crinkled.

Prompt: Get silly

in no wise simple

Alex Inaudi

in no wise simple

knowing's the prize
over ignorant's
sill ever borne

as
unity's sprawl
conflict's mesh
imbalance's poise
clarity's shade

meanings
coalesce

simple's mere shift
draping knotty truth's
twisted nethers

Prompt: The simple truth

Key

Alex Inaudi

Treasures, secrets
in safety's keep
beyond threshold

Jailer ear cocked
aching for one
unique whisper

Pocket brass charm
drawn out jangling
wielded en garde

Talisman's straight
crooked-tooth smile
speaks true, twists free

Prompt: Visual: A key

Alex Inaudi

Alex Inaudi (poet, mostly) enjoys rash gambols on the boundless upslope of art, and occasionally registers a lingering echo within whispers of transience. The writing happens daily in small journals, longhand and double-spaced, with a totemic Jetstream RT. Loved ones, their ears smiling, are generous with unfailing support. In the company of such talented fellow writers here, Alex is keenly grateful.

Words of Encouragement

"Practice writing, ideally every day." Familiar and sound advice that can be hard to follow—unless the daily efforts can be failures! So let go of quality. Ramble, be boring, make a mess. Ignore the maybe-someday reader. Those can be stumbling blocks that thwart what's essential: to make a habit of the practice.

Chuckstable

Lynn Levy

Dana cracked her gum and then smoothed it against the roof of her mouth. She pushed her tongue through, making that all-important thin membrane that would become the bubble, and Bobby watched, thinking that the gum made her tongue look as pink as the boa she was wearing. Which was saying a lot.

There was no explaining, really, why Dana was wearing a boa at all, but Bobby knew her better than to ask. Dana had on a boy's tank top, cut-off jeans, and Goodwill Kiva sandals with one of the straps broken. She also had a scab on her left knee that grossed out the toughest kid in the neighborhood, and a thin white scar on her right arm from the time she'd fallen out of the big old oak on a dare that she could climb higher than the boys. The bone had stuck through, but Dana didn't cry. After that she made her own rules, and nobody stopped her. If she wanted to wear a pink boa to catch snapping turtles, that's what she did.

Dana blew the bubble and popped it, and used her tongue to pull the broken film back into her mouth.

Bobby pushed his old safari hat down over his forehead, hoping the shadow would hide his eyes. If Dana caught him staring, he was sure he'd shrivel up and die, though he wasn't sure why. He wasn't even sure why he was staring, actually, it was just that over this last summer, somehow Dana had gotten really ... interesting.

While he watched, she took a couple of quick lithe leaps across the flat stones, until she was in the middle of the creek, cool water riding over her feet, making the creek surface a different shape right there, two smooth glassy bumps that no longer looked like feet. Dana crouched and looked down into the water. She let her fingers dangle just below the surface, the current drawing little wakes around each one. She didn't seem to notice the ends of the boa dipping into the creek, the feathers shrinking with wet.

Bobby jumped a little when she squealed. "It's a big one!" she called. Then, annoyed, "Are you gonna come help me or what?"

Bobby ambled over to the creek bank as if he was just himself, instead of how he felt, like he was someone meeting Dana for the first time and shy because of it. He'd known Dana since their Mommas had let them play out in front of the trailers, in undershirts and no pants.

"What do you want with them snappers, anyway?" Bobby asked.

"I wanna put one in Duane's outhouse," she said. "On accounta what he said about Chuckstable."

Chuckstable was Dana's dog and the love of her life. He was also the ugliest thing God ever put together. What Duane had said was actually pretty funny, but didn't bear repeating unless you liked the taste of soap.

"His Pa finds it, he'll just kill it," Bobby said. Dana looked up at him, squinting. The light caught her eyes, and the browns and greens flickered just like the creek bottom.

"Ya think?" Dana asked.

"Uh huh," Bobby said.

Dana sighed, and leaned forward, reaching into the water to stroke the turtle's shell once, carefully, from behind. Bobby noticed the way the knobs of her spine pushed against the tank top, and had the weird thought that she'd be safer in life if she had a shell too.

"You're right," she said, standing. The wet ends of the boa came out of the water and clung around her knees. "But it was fun to think about."

———————————

Prompt: Feather boa

Gabe and Andy

Lynn Levy

Gabe and Andy were five and three, and Gabe was a man of the world.

Gabe knew how to fill the water in the bird's cage, stepping down from the stool at the kitchen sink and walking carefully, never spilling a drop.

Gabe knew that wasps would sting, but that honey bees almost never did, and that it was important to leave the gray-brown pods hanging from the elm tree alone, because one day a butterfly would come out, slick and rolled up like the morning paper, and the sun would iron its wings flat and it would clap gently away—but only if you left it alone. Gabe knew which rubber duck changed color in the hot bath, and all the words to "Twinkle, Twinkle Little Star." Gabe had learned all these things by paying attention. He filled his world with the everything of everything, until sometimes he thought his head would burst with the knowing and the wonder and he would have to close his eyes to make space. The one thing Gabe did not do was let the world back out. No one knew what Gabe knew because Gabe never spoke of it. He could not fit the hugeness of the real into the tight, tight cocoon of words. It would be like trying to shove the butterfly back inside. It would break the world.

Andy was born talking. He came to the world of air with a scream of triumph and had not shut up since. Andy was the one thing Gabe had not yet figured out, but somehow, the opposite was not true.

"Gabe wants white milk, not chocolate," Andy would lisp to their mother, and Andy would be right. While Gabe could not escape Andy's usefulness, he was not sure if Andy's words would tie him up one day. What would he do if Andy was wrong?

But when he stared at Andy, Andy always smiled. He took Gabe's hand and whispered, "Say my name."

Prompt: Bird cage

Great Blue

Lynn Levy

He was Jasmine's secret. He was tall, as tall as her now, though at the beginning of the winter he might have been taller. She hoped that meant she had grown, and not that he had shrunk. She didn't know what it would mean if he had shrunk, but it probably wouldn't be good.

She'd found him that first day huddled in the middle of the field of shaggy Shetland ponies, in the middle of the huddle they made to stay warm. She'd gone out on the tractor just before dawn to spread hay and make sure the water wasn't frozen in the trough, and break the ice if it was. The ponies spread at the sound of the tractor, the way they did, and they opened like a curtain on the heron—a blue-grey slate that nearly vanished against the pre-dawn half-light.

The ponies trotted toward her, and the heron froze, then hopped away—hopped dragging one bad leg and one drooping wing. It was too far north and too far from water to be explained.

But it was too beautiful to be left. As the ponies' heat dissipated, the heron began to shiver.

Jasmine watched it from the corner of her eye while she spread the hay, and it watched her back. When she was done, she walked right up to it, and it stood stock still, and met her eye.

The bird's eyes looked black from a distance, but in the dawning half-light, Jasmine realized they were not. It was the pupil, dilated in the darkness, a ring of yellow around it, perfectly circular.

He was big, but light, and didn't struggle when she lifted him and carried him back to the tractor, setting him onto the little trailer that carried the hay.

The hen house was her next chore anyway. A heron was no hen, but the hen house was more of a barn, and she thought he'd fare better there, with his distant relatives, than with the ponies.

It takes a lot of fish to feed a heron, but she got up all winter and slogged to the river before her chores, and when the thaw came, she took him there to fish for himself. He had stayed in the copse of trees by the river into summer, prancing his tip toe ballet, swinging his beak like a pendulum, stretching his neck like a ballerina, and then, in his most graceless move, jerking the fish down his gullet. Sometimes he stood very still, watching Jasmine watching him from her perch on the rock, both of them still as statues. No one had found him. No one else went there.

He turned scraggly and bedraggled in spring and she worried he might be sick, but it was just the molt, and then he grew new feathers, sleek and smooth, and the drooping wing looked more and more normal.

It was early autumn, the leaves just starting to turn, the first time the heron walked up to her. He had never shied from her when she came near, and stared back with first one eye, and then, with a flick, suddenly the other, but he never approached her.

For the first time, he picked his fastidious high-stepping way toward her and stopped in front of where she stood, standing still for a long time.

He was a wild thing, she understood, and had never touched him since that first day on the tractor. She had not tamed him. But something compelled her to reach out and stroke the smooth feathers on his wing and back, then with one finger, the top of his head. He dipped into a little bow, and spread the wing, now well healed. Then he backed up, and with a few enormous flaps, rose into the sky and away.

Jasmine met her father walking across the field as she headed back toward the house to help fix supper.

"It's the darndest thing," her Dad said as they neared, "but I think I just saw a great blue heron fly right over the farm."

Jasmine only smiled.

Inspired by the poem "Hope and Love" by Jane Hirschfield

Javier's Last Worry

Lynn Levy

Javier lived in a box. He was just under an inch tall, which was pretty typical for his people, though he hadn't seen any of them for some time.

People could be careless with magic, especially children, who believed it so well that they sometimes made it too strong.

Mattie was five, and old enough to have quite an imagination, so Javier's life, of late, had been a little unusual.

Javier belonged to a race known as the Worry-people. Built out of twigs and bright thread, the Worry-people were stronger than they seemed. Placed beside a slumbering human, they carried worries away. The power of dreams opened the gate into another place, and the Worry-people carried the worries over and left them there, like an inter-dimensional midden heap. Worries were stories to the people who had them, but they were tangible things to the Worry-people, and could look like anything; a prickly ball, like pollen under a microscope, a bead of glass, a tangled net, a bottomless funnel, a giant hammer. Whatever the shape, Javier carried the worry away beyond dreamland and left it behind.

Until Mattie. He'd never been left to the care of a child before. Mattie didn't dream much while she slept, she mostly did it while she was awake. Her mother laughed and praised Mattie's imagination. But Javier knew better. Mattie's imagination had sent his whole clan into realms from which they could not return. Javier was the last of his kind in this house.

Isabella had been the first to vanish. Mattie had pasted little pink wings to her back, and thrown her skyward again and again. Adults would say that Isabella had gotten stuck in the rafters, but Javier had seen her transform into the fairy of Mattie's imagination, and fly away.

Jose had been marched around on the backs of toy rams and cows and even an elephant once, until he'd left with a wandering cowhand. Adults would say that Mattie had hidden Jose in the cowhand's hatband, because she had a little crush on him, but Javier knew Jose was not Jose anymore.

Lupe had spent so much time with the depthless glass marbles that Mattie imagined were gemstones that she had become trapped, in her essence, inside the glass paperweight on Mattie's dresser. Adults would say Mattie had just opened the little cork and placed her inside to be part of the decorations, but Javier knew she would never come out.

And so it went. Jorge and Sophia and Gabriella and Hector. All lost to flights of imagination.

It seemed that worry was a tethered thing; no matter how much his people disposed of, enough of it remained to keep them anchored. But Mattie's imagination flew away; vivid and real, then vapor-thin, then gone. Javier was lonely, and he was his own worry, and that was why he stayed.

Prompt: Visual: Many toys (toy animals, cat's eye marbles), random items, and a box for worry-people that contained only a single doll.

With the Top Down

Lynn Levy

Carla was 82 when she finally bought a convertible. It was a tiny little Geo, three cylinders, and had once been yellow, but yellow paint was fast to fade, and the car was almost 30 years old.

Truth was, Carla didn't have a license anymore. She was still spry and fit and had all her wits, but her eyesight was a bit lacking.

She'd wanted a convertible since she'd been in her twenties, and learned too late in life that that was exactly when she should have bought one. The responsible young tend to miss a lot of their youth, adopting too soon the weighty calculus of their parents' mortgage and college-savings priorities; putting off life until later, when they're making a bit of money, after a little more is put away, when they've seen to their obligations.

The truth was a little MG wouldn't have cost her all that much more than the used Ford she drove through college and her first job, and she'd have wrung a lot more joy out of it.

Carla's great-granddaughter was in on the scheme. She had two years of high school left and her heart set on UCLA. She'd already hired on to be Carla's chauffeur, for $10 an hour and driving privileges on the weekends, as soon as she got her license.

That wasn't for a few months, though. Today, she and Carla parked in the driveway with the top down and her Dad's biggest pedestal fan, the huge one he used to vent the garage when he painted, set up in front of them. A long orange extension cord snaked back into the gloom.

Carla's great-granddaughter fired up the fan and jumped in over the closed door like in an old movie. Carla handed her a filmy scarf, and they both practiced flipping them around their necks so that the scarves caught the roaring breeze of the fan. They made zooming noises like toddlers and laughed like idiots.

Prompt: Inspired by the poem "Grandfather's Cars" by Robert Phillips

Lynn Levy

Lynn Levy lives in Petaluma, CA, works in the software business, and loves children's literature and cats. She's been told by her friends that her childhood memories are bizarrely early and vivid. She hopes to write fiction someday that makes kids happy and thoughtful, and reminds grownups that even tiny children see themselves as people first, and kids second, and they are really busy figuring out how life works.

Words of Encouragement

For many years, I wanted to write something, a story or book, but was waiting for that great idea. When I began writing at Jump Start I learned an amazing thing. The idea doesn't come first, the writing does. You have to push the pencil to prime the pump. Just start!

Gampi

Cheryl Moore

When his wife told David that she'd invited Joan and Susan, the daughters of his deceased oldest cousin, to Sunday lunch he asked, "Why'd you do that?"

"We need to keep up family connections. And don't bring up politics or religion," Ellen warned him when she saw his scowl.

He didn't feel any need to keep up connections. What could he talk about to these young women still in their seventies, Susan a practicing Catholic and Joan a believer in Scientology. At 99 he was interested in science and the environment not in any religion that didn't believe in facts.

When Joan and Susan arrived promptly at one o'clock he glanced at Ellen and made himself say a few words of welcome. He was conscious of his stomach growling and wondered how long before she'd be putting lunch on the table. Susan followed Ellen to help in the kitchen while Joan sat close beside him on the sofa so she could talk into his good ear. She described the damage the winter's heavy rains had done to the family ranch. As Joan rambled on David vividly recalled his grandfather's ranch, tucked up in a valley surrounded by coastal hills, where he'd spent his childhood summers. He pictured the raging waters pouring down and flooding the meadow where his grandfather had kept a small herd of Jersey cows.

Summer time he and his friends had roamed up and down the hills, playing cowboys and Indians, looking for arrowheads, and watching deer, turkeys, pheasant and smaller critters. On hot afternoons they escaped to the coolness of the redwoods to play hide and seek, until his mother or one of his aunts banged on the huge triangle on the porch that served as a dinner bell.

David heard Joan's voice again and wanted to pull out his pocket watch but thought it might appear rude.

Finally Ellen called them. Leaning on his walker he made his way slowly to the head of the table. He picked up his fork to dig into the food on his plate but his wife stayed his hand. "Susan would like to say grace."

Grace? Had someone else arrived? He glanced around. Oh, that grace. He put down the fork—he hadn't heard anyone bless a meal in years.

He couldn't hear but a word or two of the conversation flowing around him. When he finished eating and sat back in his chair the women were looking at him.

"What do you remember about JK?" Joan asked him in a carefully enunciated voice.

He frowned, JK was his grandfather, "Well, you've probably heard everything already."

"You were closer to him than our mother." Susan urged, "We'd like you to tell us what you remember."

David rolled his napkin ring between his fingers and the table a few times, concentrating on the smooth motion, then looked up, "Gampi was born on a farm in the state of Maine. When the Civil War started up he was too young but tried to sign up like his older brothers. He got measles and was sent home."

"When did he come to San Francisco?" Joan asked.

David folded his napkin and inserted into its ring. Did she want an exact date? "Well, it was when he was grown up and married. He taught Latin at Lowell High School."

"But I thought he was a vice president at Wells Fargo," Joan queried.

"That was later." He looked down at the napkin still in his hands and push it aside, was she going to question everything he said?

"David, continue your story," Ellen urged.

"When did he buy the ranch?" Susan asked.

He smiled, they seemed to be interested.

"I don't rightly know, it was before I was born." He continued, "Gampi wanted a place for the family to get away from the city's foggy summers. A hired man ran the place. It was where he taught me to shoot jackrabbits. He hung their pelts on his cabin wall."

David turned to them, "You remember the cabins, don't you? Each family had one, your family, ours, Aunt Marie, and Uncle Horace."

Susan and Joan nodded.

He was getting tired and wanted to take his nap and took out his pocket watch and set it on the table.

"Later," he continued more slowly, "when I was in my teens busy with my motorcycle and my friends, I didn't see him so much. Then one day my mother came to the high school and got me out of class. She said, "Gampi needs you.""

She didn't say much as we drove to the Pacific Avenue house. She just said Gampi was sick and she thought he'd like to have me visit. She was usually very chatty, but not that day.

"She took me into his bedroom. It was hot and smelly. Gampi was propped up on pillows and seemed to be sleeping. Your mother and Aunt Marie were standing by the bed. My mother leaned close to his ear and said, "Davy's here." She placed my hand in his. I felt a slight squeeze;

I squeezed back, "Gampi?" I saw his lips twitch, then his grasp loosened."

David saw Joan wipe her eye. Maybe he shouldn't have ended the story on this sad note but at his age, older now than Gampi had been, he often thought about endings. He looked at Ellen who also had tears in her eyes. He smiled at her, "I'll tell more cheerful stories next time, but isn't it time for dessert now?"

Prompt: It's later than you think

Laundry Day

Cheryl Moore

I visited my Aunt Lonnie in Chicago when I was on vacation from school. She had a clothes washer in her basement and I enjoyed her wash day ritual. The stairs to the basement were narrow and steep. She dragged the wicker basket full of dirty clothes behind her as she held on to the railing. She loaded the washer separating the whites from the colors. Each washed with its own kind—hot water for the whites, cooler water for the colors. Then she began cranking. I was tall enough to see the pair of paddles swishing the clothes back and forth. The water splashed, sucked and swirled, like a miniature storm on Lake Michigan. The monotonous, rhythmic sound was hypnotic and soon my eye lids grew heavy. The book under my arm dropped with a plop. Aunt Lonnie laughed at me then wiped her brow and begin cranking again.

When the clothes were washed to her satisfaction, the soapy water was replaced with clean water and the cranking started again for a shorter time. I didn't stick around to watch the entire process but I came back after the rinse to watch my favorite part. She lifted out each sopping piece and stuffed it through a pair of rollers attached to the side of the washer. I liked to watch the water squeezing out and running down the side of the basin like a tiny waterfall.

She carried the basket out to the back yard where she had strung clothes lines. On rainy or very cold days the lines were strung across one end of the basement. I always liked out-of-doors better—the laundry smelled fresher. Piece by piece she pegged each to the line with wooden clothes pins, the peg kind, not the ones with a metal hinge. I liked to play with them, their round tops forming a head set atop two long curved legs. When I slipped a ring of hollyhock petals over them I had a set of ballet dancers.

Aunt Lonnie used a system to hang the clothes—no doubling over, no crowding. The air must circulate she told me. And each piece needed to be pegged securely. Otherwise a breeze could blow them off the line and make them all dirty again.

If it was a hot day, the clothes could dry in a couple of hours, time I spent playing with my cousins' toy soldiers or reading my book. If rain threatened, my aunt rushed out to bring everything in to rehang in the basement.

When the laundry was dry Aunt Lonnie showed me how to neatly fold each piece back into the basket. She brought the load into the kitchen where she spread pieces needing to be ironed out on the kitchen table. Then she filled an old coke bottle with warm water. A few holes were punched in its cap. She used this to dampen each piece, paying especial attention to collars and cuffs. Some women added another step— starch, but Aunt Lonnie preferred comfort to stiffness.

When all the clothes had been dampened she opened a tall narrow cupboard on the back porch and pulled down the ironing board. It was covered in several layers of canvas. She heated the iron on her range. When hot enough but not too hot she tested it gingerly on an old handkerchief to make sure it didn't leave a brown scorch spot. Each piece of clothing was stretched out over the board and pressed. The pressed pieces were slipped onto hangers and hooked over the kitchen curtain rod to dry. The process of heating, testing, and pressing was repeated over and over again. Finally, when she finished the last piece, she put her hands on her hips and leaned backwards to stretch.

I helped to put the freshly laundered and pressed pieces back into their proper drawers, cupboards, or closet. My aunt put away the iron and the board. Then she put the kettle on and we sat for a cup of tea, black for her, peppermint for me. She patted me on the back and said, "Well done."

There is something very endearing remembering my aunt's weekly laundry chore. It was so different from the effortless electric washer and dryer my mother had at our house out in the suburbs. Perhaps it is just my fantasy that life was simpler back then without the continual buzz and hum of electric appliances, perhaps it is just a sweet memory of a golden childhood.

Prompt: Wood clothespin

Rieke's Café

Cheryl Moore

M y mother and I came to San Francisco to start a new life. She couldn't find a job right away so as soon as I turned sixteen I applied for a Social Security card. My first job was a mother's helper for two-year-old twins. I cared for them after school every day except Thursdays when I volunteered as a candy striper at Children's Hospital. I planned to major in nursing when I went to college.

When the twin's family moved away one of my teachers told me about a small deli needing a waitress. Rieke's Café was on Polk Street, two doors down from Blum's. I was hired immediately and showed up for work the next day in my new white uniform, white comfortable shoes, and a small white cap, with a bit of imagination I looked like a nurse. I worked four to nine weekdays and noon to nine on Saturdays earning the minimum wage, $1.25 per hour, tips were miniscule.

A high counter ran along one side of the long narrow interior. Under its slanted glass front was a patchwork of shapes—rounds and cylinders of sausages; blocks and wheels of cheeses in assorted sizes—chunks of feta, balls of mozzarella, and holy Swiss—and great bowls of freshly made salads and slaws. Behind the counter were shelves of colorful liquor bottles.

Running along the opposite side were eight two-person tables separated by white trellises, the décor perhaps trying to imitate the look of an outdoor garden. At each place setting stood a fancy green water goblet. The tiny kitchen was four-steps up at the back.

The owners, Mr. and Mrs. Rieke, seemed old to me but were probably late middle age. Mrs. Rieke looked like a fading actress, plump with heavily rouged cheeks, thick eye liner, and obviously dyed red hair. She wore thick glasses, usually smeared. Mr. Rieke was small and thin with receding dark reddish hair showing grey at the roots. He was kindly and serious while she was excitable. They had fled Eastern Europe before the war.

Coming from a semi-rural area of the Midwest I'd never been in a Jewish deli before and the new tastes and smells from behind the counter were wonderful—salty pastrami, rare roast beef and a variety of salamis, and desserts—sweet baklava, juicy apple and cherry strudels, accompanied with Sweet-Touch-Nee tea. Drifting above the kitchen aromas was the fragrance of strong coffee.

I learned the first Saturday that there was more to waitressing than taking orders and serving food. It was busy. Mrs. Rieke was making sandwiches but was getting behind with the orders. The customers were getting impatient so I started slapping sandwiches together to speed things up. Then a week later the dishwasher got clogged and at the end of the evening I stood with my hands in soapsuds in order to have clean dishes for the next day. If Mr. Rieke had to go to the bank or buy more groceries for the kitchen, I sliced cold cuts behind the counter.

It didn't take me long to realize that Mrs. Rieke was not a cook. The stroganoff or goulash she prepared came out of industrial size cans. She once described a room in her house which she had done up in velvet drapes and oriental rugs where she liked to sit and remember how things had been before the war. Running a small café probably wasn't how she had planned to spend her life.

Closing time and my shift were supposed to end at nine, but if a customer came in just a few minutes before, I was expected to stay until he left. The Riekes didn't pay me for this extra time but gave me a lift home which I appreciated.

I had my failings as Mr. Rieke quickly discovered when I made mistakes in adding up bills. He made sure to check my figures before diners discovered my errors. When I accidentally broke one of Mrs. Rieke's green goblets, she exploded; I thought I was going to be fired but I wasn't.

One of the regular diners was an older gentleman, a painter with a studio a couple of blocks away. After I'd been at the café awhile he showed me the numbers the Nazi had put on his lower arm. Then he asked if I could help him straighten up his studio. I liked the paintings I'd seen in his window and considered it but when I told Mr. Rieke about the idea he shook his head and advised against. Two handsome young men often came in for supper. I found one of them very attractive and did my best to be friendly, but I soon learned that gay meant something besides happy.

When I had been working there almost a year, Mr. Rieke whom I knew was fond of me explained sadly that in order to increase business he needed to apply for a beer and wine license which meant that he wouldn't be able to keep me on; I was only seventeen.

I wasn't sad to leave, my volunteer work at Children's Hospital, helped me get a ward clerk job, much more in line with my plans to be a nurse.

I visited the Riekes once a few weeks after leaving and saw the older girl they had hired to replace me. She was chewing gum, looked bored and didn't smile. Mr. Rieke told me he missed me.

A year later riding on the Polk street bus, I looked for

the familiar Rieke's Café sign but it had been replaced by the Golden Dragon. I hoped that the Riekes were comfortably retired. They deserved a rest after the long hours and hard work they put into that café. For me it was my first real job, an adventure in a memorable time. I had passed from school girl to adulthood and learned of the wider world, of life's darker side and its unpredictability, and the feeling of pride in joining the working world.

Prompt: Write about your first job.

Thanksgiving

Cheryl Moore

It was our second Thanksgiving in Tehran. My husband, Bijan, and I had come to live in his hometown more than a year before. This Thanksgiving happened to coincide with a Moslem holy day, a sad one, Ashura, which mourned the death of Imam Hussein, a grandson of the prophet Muhammad, martyred more than thirteen hundred years ago.

Our flat was directly across a narrow street from a building with a mosque on its first floor, a tailor's shop on the second, and a business office on the third. On the roof a loud speaker broadcast in Arabic, the traditional call to prayer at sunrise and sunset. Its noise blended into my days as did many other sounds—the incessant horns honking from the nearby boulevard, vendors calling out their wares of pomegranates, grapes or manure as they led their donkey or camel down our little street. The warm summer evenings brought voices of a crowd gathered in the street to buy watermelon or sizzling kebab sold by the mosque custodian.

On Thanksgiving morning while Bijan went off to play tennis, I planned to go to help my friend and co-worker, Margaret, with dinner preparations. She had invited us and a few other Americans to celebrate with her and her young son. They were on their own this holiday as her husband was in the United States finishing up his Ph.D.

I was preparing to leave the flat but hesitated when I looked out the window. Usually when the call to pray sounded, men, mostly laborers from construction sites all around the neighborhood, appeared. They took off their shoes, descended to the basement to wash their heads and feet, then climbed to the sanctuary to perform their prayers. But today was Ashura, they came carrying ropes and chains with small hooks attached and began flaying their backs in front of the mosque. They were re-enacting the death of Imam Hussein, who was trampled to death with his followers under the hooves of his foes' horses. The men were in a frenzy shouting, "Allah Akbar"—Allah is Great.

I, as a blue-eyed, blond foreigner, decided to wait before venturing out. After a while the men quieted and entered the mosque, then I made my escape.

At Margaret's house Mary, another invitee, was just leaving. She had brought cans of cranberry sauce and pumpkin pie filling purchased on her last visit to the U.S. They were her contribution to the dinner. I could tell Margaret was relieved at her departure. Margaret told me that her family back in Utah were Mormon but she didn't practice anymore and Mary, who was an active member, was critical of Margaret's lapse and hoped to get her back in the fold. Margaret felt obliged to invite her. She would return with her husband and sons when dinner was ready. Mary had quizzed her on who was invited, and when Margaret mentioned the boss Margaret and I shared at our office. Mary disapproved because his wife wouldn't be with him. His wife hadn't liked living in Tehran and had returned to the U.S. with their children.

Margaret sighed, "I don't think it very Christian to let him spend the holiday alone." I agreed.

We went into the kitchen. Our bird sat proudly in its roasting pan. Margaret opened the spigot on the gaz cylinder and turned on the oven. We waited but no flame lit. The gaz capsule was empty. We looked at each other across the open oven door. Hossein, her houseboy, had forgotten to tell her. She sent him out hoping he'd find a shop still open, in Tehran most stores closed early on Thursdays.

"We can always cut the bird up and cook it over the heat from the radiator," Margaret laughed.

"Yes," I joked, "if we want to wait eight or ten hours for it to slow cook."

We continued our preparations. She asked me to make the dinner rolls and handed me a packet of dried yeast. I noticed its expiration date was two years past. I added the yeast to warm water to test it. In the Middle East's dry climate even mummies are preserved forever so I figured it would work. "Do you have an electric frying pan?" I asked, thinking of alternatives for baking the rolls if Hossein couldn't find any gaz.

She looked at me, "Do you think this is an American kitchen?"

I shook my head and began making pastry for the pie crusts. I couldn't imagine what we would do with the canned pumpkin if we couldn't bake it into a pie. Margaret prepared the side dishes—bread stuffing, candied carrots, and broccoli, a vegetable considered exotic in Tehran, available only at the one American-style supermarket.

To our relief about four o'clock Hossein returned with the gaz. He hooked it up and we popped the turkey into the oven. Just before five Mary returned with her family. She was clearly annoyed that dinner wasn't on the table. Bijan arrived, then our boss, who brought his contribution—several bottles of Shiraz wine.

We sat around the festively decorated table eating crackers and cheese, four of us indulged in the wine. Mary and her family sat opposite drinking orange soda. Margaret tried to unite the group by asking each guest to describe their

Thanksgiving tradition back home. She got up frequently to baste the bird, letting its fragrance fill the air. By nine o'clock when the turkey was ready we wine drinkers were quite happy as we all sat down at the table.

Margaret sat at the head. Our boss chose the seat next to her and made a toast thanking her for inviting him. We toasted the turkey for sacrificing itself on this holy day in both cultures.

Mary and her family left soon after the pumpkin pie saying the children needed to go to bed. I helped Margaret clean up the kitchen, then Bijan and I took our leave.

Back at the office on Saturday morning, the start of the Iranian work week, Margaret told me that Mary stopped by early the morning after Thanksgiving. Margaret suspected that she was checking to see if our boss had spent the night.

"Well, did he?" I joked.

Margaret smiled and shook her head, "He might have if I'd invited him but I didn't."

I've had many wonderful Thanksgivings since leaving Tehran, with friends and family, and more recently with grandchildren. I've roasted a traditional turkey, served the customary side dishes and cooked it all in a conventional American kitchen but no Thanksgiving has been so exotic, so close to not happening, nor with such a mix of cultures as that Thanksgiving in Tehran.

Prompt: An unexpected or memorable holiday

The Wait

Cheryl Moore

The shrill alarm clock woke her from a dream so powerful, yet so fleeting that it was immediately banished from her memory. She tried to recapture the feeling but it was gone. She stared into the winter darkness trying to remember but not even a shadowy image remained. She glanced at the clock—it was late. She barely caught her bus before the doors closed. It was a chartered commute bus carrying the same people into the city's medical center every day. She had only started the job a few weeks before.

The bus was often crowded without enough seats for all its passengers. Those boarding at the last stop often stood in the aisle for the hour and twenty-minute journey. Today she saw an empty seat near the back and quickly slid into it. She closed her eyes waiting for her heartbeat to return to normal after the morning's rush. When she opened them she glanced at her seatmate, who looked up from his book and smiled. She felt a stirring spread through her chest. He wasn't extraordinarily good looking, his hair, what was left of it, graying, but his gray-green eyes sparkled and held hers in a sweet frankness that made it difficult for her to turn her gaze away.

After that day he saved the seat next to him for her. They shared his newspaper and after a couple of weeks discovered they enjoyed the same authors and began sharing books. One day he asked if he could take her to lunch. They rode a cable car to a small café in Chinatown where in her nervousness she nearly choked on her pot sticker.

He worked in another department but communicated through the office mail sending her his small colorful drawings of the scenes they passed on their long bus rides. During the week they sometimes met at a café, the Marigold, where one day over tea and poppy seed muffins he told her he'd like to marry her. She didn't reply knowing that he needed to first end his marriage, as did she, but she liked the idea.

When summer came they sometimes met on Saturday afternoons to paint landscapes in watercolors. After a year or so, when they were free to be together, she moved her belongings into the small bare fixer-upper he bought. They spent their weekends remodeling. When the remodeling was mostly complete, she found a job nearby and began to think about marriage. She was happy enough for the moment so didn't bring it up.

Another year passed, marriage wasn't mentioned. By this time she'd earned enough vacation to visit a former college roommate who lived in Italy. She decided this was a good time to leave him on his own and see what happened when she returned.

She had a wonderful time visiting and seeing Turin, Perugia, Venice, and Rome. She vowed to travel as much as she could no matter what happened in the future.

Upon her return he greeted her enthusiastically, telling her that he'd gone to the movies every night while she'd been away to fill the void. He showed her the new suit he'd bought and asked if there was a neighborhood church she particularly liked.

"Interesting," she thought. Neither of them were churchgoers.

After a few days he told her he'd made an appointment to see the pastor of a church a few blocks away. It was an esthetically pleasing little church and together with the pastor they chose an afternoon a month away for their wedding day. They invited a few friends. She bought a dress off the sale rack at Macy's and some groceries from the local market.

On the morning of the selected day she got up early to begin preparing refreshments. A couple of hours later a neighbor stopped by with a gift. The neighbor stood in the kitchen doorway and stared at the rolling pin poised to roll out dough, the quiche pans sitting on the counter, the flour-dusted jeans, and asked, "Aren't you getting married today?"

"Yes, I think I am," she smiled.

Prompt: Write about a dream

Cheryl Moore

Life began for Cheryl Moore in 1962 when she talked her mother into moving to San Francisco. She had seen it earlier on a family vacation, when after the hot muggy Midwest where she'd been raised, San Francisco's bright, white buildings, ocean breezes and fog racing in under the Golden Gate were etched in her memory.

Words of Encouragement

For years, I dabbled with writing short pieces but without a regular time or method. Sometimes months went by without my writing a single creative word. But since joining Marlene Cullen and Susan Bono at Jumpstart Writing Workshops, using prompts, which take the form of a poem, a phrase, sometimes a single word, or even a display of objects, my mind is stimulated to make an association or a memory, or even a crazy idea and I begin putting words down on paper and spin fresh ideas. It is a freeing session to explore whatever comes flowing out of my pen.

These weekly sessions are for anyone who has ever thought about writing, whether fiction or nonfiction, poetry or prose. It is an especially encouraging place for novices who have absolutely no writing experience and don't know where to begin. It also serves the more experienced writer who wants a safe place in a small group to sharpen their skill and to explore new ideas. These germs of ideas when worked up and polished later may be the basis of an entirely new and exciting journey to enrich a life.

Harvest

Christine Renaudin

November 14, 2016

Now, the moon looms large. Now, the amber moon pauses upon the horizon. And now, we write, in the restless public space where we choose to meet weekly, rain or shine. We write over the voice of the miked lady in the window reading stories to passers-by. In our little town, a not-so-young lady reclines on the floor, in a brightly lit window, reclaims literacy and other oral and literate delicacies for parents and their children passing by well after nightfall on their way to god knows where, her gray hair falling over her face bent over the page. Now she reads, and when she stops, she sings to fill the silence others crave to explore more delicate, adult, private, territories.

Now the moon, the plump November amber moon sits a little higher up in the sky over the town, still alert with story desires, scratching pens and silence-craving pen-pushers. We form a group. We have wings, although unlike geese, who just hours before honked their way through dusk-colored shreds of clouds, we travel sedentarily, so to speak, and we write, together and apart, tearing up imaginary hills, gliding along meandering rivers, remembered bridges, deltas and estuaries, walking under yellow streetlights through soft, foggy evenings that touch our faces as we look ahead, where the night darkens.

Now the beaver moon, we know—we have been told—will not return for another eighteen years, lifts our spirits, unfolds our spines, as if pulling skyward the tide of us.

And now the children are talking, wondering out loud at the window-trapped lady with a voice that sings off-key. They babble twice and are gone, silenced by other noises or desires. Now the children want more story, less display, and the parents gently pull them inside or out.

And the moon keeps climbing up darkness, illuminating our evening, still young, so soft we suddenly crave bursting outside to feel the fleshy touch of night on our faces, now bent upon notebooks, eyes shifting words under the tips of pens. Now we feel the moon swelling inside hearts and sinews, diffusing its unusually warm glow under our skins, into our veins. Now we write, and now we ride the post-election wave under the amber moon. We go with the flow of our tides, against unwanted shores we know now to make our own, for better and for worse.

Soon, the moon will start descending on the other side of the sky, shortly to sink below the earthly horizon, for now, though still rising ominously, ascending its luminous rotundity above our heads, a bright and warm pondering dot under oversized and hidden question marks crowding the dark space above town. Now we wonder, which flow to go along with.

Now, the crashing wave of rebellion and its powerful undertow soothes a violent desire to destroy and go back, reset the clock, erase the rush of events. Now, the surf rider prevails, and the strong stroke of the swimmer sustained and rocked by the beat of her own rhythmical effort to make her way through this shark-filled ocean coldness. Now the sands of the shore begin to make more sense.

Now they beckoned, as in beacons and bonfires, luring the lost and tired to the light of their flames, or like the deceitfully warm glow of an overgrown amber moon, now cruising over town, a faceless clock pregnant with times untold, a fancy gravid rolling stone rounding its sides against the sky, a deceptive piñata holding pledges of sweet happenings and candied stories.

Now you want to strike, break open the portentous fullness of the moon, unseal its load of poisonous promises, undo spells cast in fear, greed, and malicious provocation.

Now, the dice roll again. Now, we shall taste of the rotten apple, find the fat worm, eat it alive, make it our own until we transform it. Now, we shall find purpose.

Prompt: Inspired by the poem "The Shining Moment in the Now," by David Budbill

If Only

Christine Renaudin

If only … She said to take it from there, but I can't. Not in the mood tonight to play that game, if only because I've come to know better than bemoan the un-happened, the step not taken, or misplaced. I've learned that it does not help to regret what hasn't happened in the past. The urge to judge and flagellate, the impulse to shame and humiliate, rooted in old rough grounds sometimes obscure the terrain, hide the tenderer soil where fertile forgiveness and humility grow together likes carrots and lettuce in the same garden bed.

If I hadn't forgotten my notebook in the seat pocket of the plane that brought me home the year after I lost my mother, and if I hadn't lost my wits over it all, I most likely would not be writing here tonight the kind of stuff I've come to write on good Mondays.

If I hadn't, against my will, unwittingly abandoned that yellow diary purchased the year in France after my mother died, during that grueling time of mourning when I experienced such difficulty processing grief and anger, I might have continued covering pages with words that sustained rather than soothed the emotions I needed to channel into shaping new life, and most probably would have gone on scribbling.

If I hadn't been on sabbatical that year my mother passed, I wouldn't have had a chance to show her how much I did care for her after others had tried to impress that I didn't. She might have gone convinced that I was lost, indeed.

If my mother had not said those words when she realized I was standing at the foot of her bed, in the room where she was slowly emerging from chemo induced delirium, I wouldn't have caught on how much damage had been wrought between us in my absence, for her to say, in bitter disbelief: "Ah, you're here! I thought you were lost."

Is this how she put it? Were these the words she used? I cannot remember for sure her exact terms—sunk in translation, burned by the scathing moment that had me drop them as if red pieces of coal, branding holes in the flesh of my memory. I know I wrote them down in the yellow notebook forgone in pain and anger, for my sake.

Tonight, there is something in the music playing that keeps me from writing. Not because I find it irritating, but because I like it enough not to be able to leave it alone. It grasps my attention and won't let go, making me want to drift and dance instead of following the writing prompt. At the same time, when the music stops, so does my pen, as if it had been dancing along with the music. So is the music tonight keeping me from writing, or is it carrying me on scribbling?

Perhaps this distraction is nothing short of inspiration, perhaps it has nothing to do with the music at all, but is rather simply a matter of mood, of being sick and tired, jet lagged, dealing with a growing anxiety about a certain lack of certainty that seems to spread about practically everything every time I return from a place I still call home.

There is some real sadness in the air—even a touch of despair, if only fleetingly. You know I'd rather see the good and round of it, the carving and scooping in the negative space rather than a void. As long as there is ground to dance, emptiness sounds fine. Groundlessness, however, would be another story, and exhausting the dance attempting to bridge the gap between two homes, one foot on each land, or jumping from one to the other continuously.

Loss is real, and so is the dance of words and limbs I want to carry on sharing.

Prompt: If only . . .

Ink

Christine Renaudin

I'd like to see again the small dance of dusk making its way over the streets of my childhood on a wet winter day when the light fades fast and early, the moment the sky turns thick, ink-purplish as it darkens under street lamps, catching the drizzle in their beams and leaving streaks of liquid yellow on the black pavement all shiny with rain. I'd like to feel the surprise of the night again, fast fallen while my eyes are busy capturing lemony streams of gold in the curbs, running into the drain between pleasure and pain, loss and gain.

Prompt: Something you'd like to see again

Marie Pie Time

Christine Renaudin

M arie had a long sweet tooth. She'd add a spoonful or two of jam to the butter in her pasta. Every excuse was good enough to bake a cake, make a charlotte, cook a pie, every birthday, every family member's patron saint's day. We had many of those in June, July and August, and summer was pie season heralded by the monumental, unforgettable strawberry custard pie with its fleshy, pointy seeded cones standing covered in lustrous glaze on homemade crust, knee deep in yellow buttery sweetness. Children loved it; adults, glad for seconds, willingly went along with ritual. "I'd better make two just in case," she'd say. "Leftovers won't stay long in the safe."

When the grandchildren grow up and leave town, she'll grow tired of baking victories, and even of the taste of pies. It will be time to quit and sit with her hands folded on her lap, eyes lost above the horizon, through the wall and beyond into undecipherable mists of past and present dreameries nobody will suspect in an old woman so quiet, dignified and seemingly so patient.

Nevertheless someone eventually will drop by on the chair next to her, and it will take a moment for her to register this new presence and the expectation of attention. She will gently turn her head and politely smile to the newcomer. It will take another moment to make sense of the visitor's sentence, let her voice sufficiently penetrate the fog of lingering reveries for recognition to mark the intersection of past and present, memory and perception. Only then will a wave of warmth suddenly flood her crystalline, almost childish peals of laughter as the familiar name of her granddaughter crosses her lips several times. The sound it makes is a delight, the sight of her womanly face a wonder. And you wouldn't know from their now joined voices who is the younger of the two; only the granddaughter can say that in pie time, it's not hers.

Let them stay inside the tiled, overheated waiting room, where the double doors regularly swing open, letting in rushes of cold air to dispel some of the cooking odors wafting from the kitchen floor below. Let them wait for lunch together by the maroon painted wainscot, holding each other's hands in happy disbelief. Let them laugh and recall sweet nothings. "I don't have much to tell you, you know. Nothing interesting ever happens here, and I can't really follow conversations anymore."

Let them mock the circumstances. Let the younger one see the fading color in the older one's gaze, the pale blue halo circling the iris that used to shine as brown as a chestnut caught in the rain. "Everything goes too fast for me now, you know. It's overwhelming." Let the older one complain and the younger commiserate. "Mrs. B. is a thief, you know. I've had to hide my things." Let the drama unfold of imaginary thefts or menial and invented crimes. The truth is that she no longer has anything to hide or keep—no key, no safe, no secret space for stored mementos of other lives. She has given it all—the stiff and yellowed home-sewn night shirts and underwear of her trousseau; the houses, the postcards, letters and photographs, recipes written on the run on a piece of cardboard torn from an empty package of corn flour, the corner of an envelope, a sheet of an old school workbook of mine. She's on her own entirely, left to her last devices and the whims of her memory. They come to her, dictate her meandering thoughts, take her on trips she wouldn't have dreamed of ever taking when she was constantly running out of time. Now she can err all she wants, although sometimes she does not and would prefer absolute stillness of the mind. Now time moves through her freely, filling her with stories, lived or imagined, mostly a bit of both, forgotten and fleetingly recaptured, suddenly turned captivating. She goes from one to the other in no chronological order, following a path ever renewed that takes her far away from pies other people now make for her with a lot less passion she used to put in hers. She's done criticizing them. She eats them without a complaint, mostly with a straight face, enjoying those last bites of sweetness with the gratefulness of wisdom.

The missing piece might be a sieve to pass the stories through the test of truth, sort out the real from the rest consistently thrusting itself against the familiar grain with a force so great, so constant she finds herself trusting it as the very texture of her days, the tether that keeps her going inside in spiraling journeys where sights already seen, facts long ago recorded, unexpected crossings and intersections, meandering detours of meaning she never tires of following since time has come to be irrelevant, get her lost and retrieved in turn again and again. Yet she keeps counting the years, does not miss the missing piece, and her granddaughter does not either.

Prompt: Inspired by the poem "The Poet's Occasional Alternative" by Grace Paley

Thursday rains

Christine Renaudin

"Don't just sit there sifting away the day," she'd say, when she found me idling by the window sill, tracing paths in the dust. "Pick up a rag and clean!"

—And I'd start dreaming of a white duster to wear in some desert under the rain.

"Don't let the turntable idle and sing its broken seesaw! Start the record again, or put it away!"

—I'd pick up a needle, and sew silly patterns on a slippery sleeve.

"Don't put your dirty hands on the clean fabric I just set on the sewing-machine," she'd warn, a bit too loud. "Read your book and learn something useful!"

—So I'd rummage in the pantry, feeling each box for its content of spices, sugar, and chocolate.

"Have a piece!" She'd throw me a bone.

—I'd reach into the wrapper, bring the dark and sweet bitterness to my mouth, wrap my tongue around it and start thinking of a white Christmas.

"Won't snow in our neck of the woods. Too soft, too wet."

—"But when," I'd ask, "do you use the thermos bottle you keep far and deep on the bottom shelf?"

"Not until our chickens grow teeth," she'd laugh. "Urchin."

—Then, in a fog, I knew to trust dust, fingers, tongue, and the patterns up a sleeve.

Prompt: Write about the objects displayed: a flour sifter, a vinyl record and its sleeve, a bit of fabric, a Christmas card, a thermos bottle.

Christine Renaudin

Christine lives, writes, and paints in Petaluma, CA. She is also a dancer and performs occasionally in the Bay Area. She likes to mix art forms and makes a living teaching literature, creativity, and performance.

Words of Encouragement

Do it! Do it in secret or in the open, do it with your heart. Share what you care to share and process the rest into more writing, or painting, or dancing, or living your everyday life. Don't worry too much about a final product, there isn't one, even when you call a piece done and, say, publish it. It could always be refined, rewritten. Get on to something and pursue it as many times, in as many ways as it takes it for you to feel done with it—for a while, at least—decide if and what you want to share, when and how, and start a new one.

Her Things

Su Shafer

He lies in the darkness surrounded by her things.
They watch him, how his eyes close, then open again
Close, then open again, searching the room for something
Lost or maybe something safe to hold onto.
Her things creep closer to his bed
Hover over his sweating form.
They breathe hot disapproval and accusations
"If you had only done this," they whisper.
"Why didn't you? Why didn't you? Why didn't you?"
Their anger is thunder in his ears.
They are her ghosts, reminders that haunt and
Torment him in the ink-still hours.
In the morning, they recede like shadows
And wait sullenly for nightfall.
He rises, still bent beneath the cast-iron weight
Of a nightmare that has no waking.

Prompt: Inspired by the poem "Things" by Lisa Mueller

My Right Hand

Su Shafer

I don't like shaking hands.
My right-hand, numb as a stranger,
Is forgetful and untrustworthy.
I have to watch it to know what it is doing
I hold my breath, nervous as a mother
whose child has wandered out of sight
when it disappears in the clutches of another hand
during the courtesy of a handshake.
My mind is directing it to clasp the strange hand
normally, if lightly, but I'm never sure
what it's actually doing.
Is it a claw?
Are the fingers all bent up in a crooked fist?
Is it laying there like a stiff salami?
Are my nails digging in?
Is my middle finger doing something naughty?
I watch the stranger's face for clues
of any right-handed misbehaviors
and exhale with relief when my hand is released.
This is their first impression of me —
I will never know what my right hand just told them.

Prompt: Inspired by the poem "What I Like and Don't Like"
by Philip Schultz

Nodie's Farmhouse

Su Shafer

Tomey lived up the holler from me about a mile or so, but her house was about as far apart from our little farm as a place could be. We were best friends almost as soon as my dad moved us to the little fixer-upper hobby farm in the back wood hills of West Virginia. Tomey's ma, Nodie, owned 500 acres further back in the hills and let the mining company strip them bare. Rounding the last bend of the little dirt road, the site of their farm hit you real sudden and just made you want to turn back. All the sheltering woods had been ripped away as far as the eye could see, leaving behind something scarred and terrible to behold. Their farmhouse sat like a scab in the middle of all of that skinned land, the dirt all around as orange and sulfurous as a butchered cow. I remember thinking even as a child of nine, that life here was as stripped down as the land around it.

The house stood and gaped at the road like some old hill person with a rotting smile. An old fire from "a long time ago" they said, had left a lot of damage to the front. The charred walls, like old blackened gums, surrounded the vacant holes where doors and windows used to be, and gave the face of the house a sad, almost haunted, countenance. And it had bad breath, too, that house, exhaling the odors of an interior left alone to fester despite its many inhabitants. You could smell it coming up the walk. The air inside sank dead and hovered low over the floor, heavy with the stench of mold and burnt things and overflowing toilets. I had to cover my nose so I wouldn't gag, but even pinching it hard didn't stop that barfy stink from turning the grilled cheese in my stomach upside down and over sideways.

But for all of that, there was something kindly about it too, and I wasn't afraid. Maybe it was that all the folk there were happy to see me and show me around. Tomey had three sisters, plus her pa and grandpa. And of course, Nodie herself was there too, working and swearing underneath her old pick-up truck which was rocking back and forth over her bulk like it was stranded on a boulder. Nodie was a BIG woman. Not fat-big, burly-big. Legendary, like Paul Bunyan. She had shoulders like all the West Virginia hills were stuffed inside her white undershirt, the hilltops and valleys rolling in her muscles as she moved. She mostly wore coveralls, man-style, with her name stitched in a little oval patch on her chest. High cheekbones made her black eyes squinty and mean looking, and though Nodie looked like a big beefy man that a grizzly bear wouldn't want to tangle with, you'd sure want her on your side in any kind of tussle. She had a quick, hearty laugh that offset her brawny impact, and an easy-going manner that let you know she was a straight shooter and would do right by you if she counted you as a friend. My dad took to her the minute she roared up our steep driveway on her motorbike to welcome her new neighbors. Her hair was pomaded into a slick pompadour and when she shook my dad's hand, it disappeared inside her fist like a little china doll's. He immortalized her in a painting riding that bike, its two wheels bowed up underneath the crushing weight of that enormous Himalayan she-Elvis. He called it "Mountain Woman." And that's what she was. A mountain of a woman.

I only went to their farmhouse just the one time. And once I'd been to that blistered place where everything was peeled and raw, I never went back, though our friendship kept going until my family moved away back to the city. But that farmhouse haunts me a little. For all its burned and stinky ruin, that house was a survivor. Somehow it just hung on.

Before that day, I never thought about poverty and neglect. We weren't rich on my dad's teacher salary, but more than money, we seemed to have something tangible that they didn't. The mining company should have paid Nodie a lot of money to strip her land for coal, but I couldn't make sense of a place where even the youngest kid had a motorcycle but not a real bed to sleep in or even a front door to close. My dad said the mining company picked the land and Nodie's family clean down to their bones. But I think maybe after a lifetime of having nothing she didn't know she could have anything else.

Prompt: Write about someone from your childhood.

Storm

Su Shafer

I am awake even as the cat sleeps
She is like a solid little ship of dreams
Bobbing and floating on a stormy sea of blankets
Cottony turbulence caused by my tossing and turning
There is a noise inside me
Loud as a streetlight shining directly on the inside of my
  eyelids
Sleep is not an option
He is far away sleeping with someone else
And this fury of light he awakened
Is raging and stamping like a mustang in a stall
If I could unleash these feelings
Send them galloping over the plains like a rolling storm
Shake the walls of his house with the thunder of my heart
Pelt his windows with a stabbing rain of words and
  frustration
Let him shiver in the darkness as I shiver in this light
This relentless brightness that won't let me sleep.

Prompt: In the middle of the night

The Capriciousness of Hormones

Su Shafer

My hormones are partying like rock stars on a farewell tour,
Completely trashing this joint
Puberty was a cake walk —
A skip through the park on a sunny spring day,
Birds singing in the trees, flowers blooming in the grass.
Now I am in the Halloween season of my body.
It took years of careful honing for my hormones
To learn these tricks and apply them with precision
The way a needle might be pushed under a fingernail just so
A confession is beside the point.
I'm a volcanic stew of burbling anger/giddiness/depression/
    hope
Hot as the surface of the sun / bone chilled as Pluto's
    distant heart.
There is a knife in my hand as I sob over a dog food
    commercial.
Why am I having cramps when I have no uterus?!
Because the body never forgets and my lower back
Still mourns the loss of its buddy.
My ovaries, sad and doomed, play on and on,
Like the band on the Titanic—yes that's me
Upended and going down …
…
Sorry, I lost my train of thought. What was I saying?

*Prompt: Inspired by the poem "The Sadness of Ice Cream"
by Ron Salisbury*

Su Shafer

Su Shafer was creating stories and poems even before she could pick up a pencil. She draws as naturally as she writes and her doodles are often sketches of a larger story internally unfolding. Sensitive to the living energy in every object, be it rock, twig, or tea kettle—any and all are colorful characters in her world. She recently heeded the call of the Pacific Northwest and moved into the little Baba Yaga house that was waiting for her near The Hidden Wood. At night the trees dance and the frogs sing to her, "Write-write, write-write!"

Words of Encouragement

Beware the trap that writers often fall into: The Inner Critic Tar Pit of Doom and Despair—the black hole of fear in your head that says you have nothing new or exciting to say or that even if you are personally excited by what you've written, it's not good enough for someone else to read or hear.

It's a creative quicksand that will sink the soul right out of your writing, further feeding the fear of mediocrity. The only way to escape this pit is to get out of your head. I've found doing timed free writes is a great way to do this.

When your time is restricted, you don't have time to obsess over a word or a phrase and there simply isn't enough time to polish. There is something freeing and reassuring about that. And having a time limit ensures that you can't get too invested and that what goes on the paper is raw, organic, and unraveled from the sinister inner critic with its conformist ideals.

Play, don't be afraid to experiment. Use creative prompts to catapult you out of your comfort zone. Don't try to control or stop what wants to come out. It's surprising and delightful what valuable nuggets and insights show up.

Be brave and share your work with others. Other people come to your writing with their own perspectives and will often pull things from your writing that wouldn't otherwise occur to you. Sharing your work is the only way to get over your fear of sharing your writing. And when you're not too invested, you can accept both complements and criticism and learn to use them constructively. Most importantly, just keep writing. Do whatever it takes—invent ways to keep your pen scribbling on paper. Just keep writing.

All the Little Savages

Jo-Anne Rosen

It was a pleasure to be out on the open road with Arnold now that he'd quit drinking while driving. They were both tickled with the new rig. It was an azure-blue Dodge camper with stick shift, which he'd insisted on, though he knew she couldn't drive it. She had picked the color though and the accessories. It had a cunning miniature kitchen and the table made into a bed.

"Where to?" he asked. "The coast or the mountains?"

"Let's head for the hills."

"Anywhere you want, sugar, just say the word."

If only that were true, she thought, and opened the map.

His window was rolled down and his fine hair lifted in the breeze. There was only a bit of gray in it. Darcy patted her new perm uneasily. Was the color too obvious? Lately she had been feeling her age.

"Did Taylor say when dinner is?" she asked.

"Sixish. We've got all afternoon free."

"Who else'll be there?"

He grinned. "All the little Savages."

"What if we didn't show up," she said slowly. "Just this once?"

"Why, honeybunch, whatever are you thinking?"

"That Taylor is so bossy and critical. I'd like to see her face if we phoned and said, oh I don't know what, like we're on our way to the Grand Canyon. Whose anniversary is it, anyway?"

"She only wants to please us. She's a sweet little thing."

Darcy ignored that. Their son had married a divorcee and settled in Eugene, a two-hour drive to the north. Junior and Taylor Savage had six children total, four from previous marriages. Taylor ran the house like an army camp. It gave Darcy a headache to visit. But Arnold always had a good time there. No wonder, the size of the bourbons Taylor poured him. Then they'd have to sleep over on the sofabed. Till now.

"I thought we might go out for a special dinner instead, some place really different, just you and me."

"We always go up to Eugene Sundays." He looked genuinely puzzled. "You like to visit the grandkids, don't you?"

"Not every blessed Sunday. Can't we do something different, just this once?"

"Like what? Drive to the Grand Canyon?"

"Why not? What's the camper for?"

"Darcy, you've got to plan a trip like that."

She thought about it.

"Okay. Here's a plan. We don't absolutely have to be anywhere for three weeks, right?"

He shrugged. "If you say so." It was Darcy who made all their appointments.

"You see the doctor in three weeks. Can you stand to skip a poker game or two?" No answer. She went on.

"So, we keep driving east. Pick up food along the way and maps. Buy a change of clothes. We call a neighbor and ask them to take in the mail and the newspaper.

"You're serious?"

"I'm serious."

He tapped the steering wheel. "You're a wild woman, Mrs. Savage. What would we tell the kids?"

"We're on a second honeymoon. Freeze the leftovers."

He put his head back and roared. She laughed, too. She felt years younger suddenly.

"Wagons, ho!" he said, and he pushed on the accelerator. "I'll drive you to the moon and back if you want. Only thing I won't do is call Taylor. She's going to be mighty peeved."

"I'll call her." Darcy took out her phone. No bars. It could wait till they got to a town. For a moment she imagined herself dealing with those six screaming hyperactive children day after day, as well she could, having raised three, herself. It could drive a woman to drink, she supposed, and she almost relented. But only for a moment. She'd never seen the other side of that mountain before, what was it called? Trout Creek Mountain. The road unwound before them up into the high desert. They were going to drive over that mountain and the next. She would drive on forever if only they could.

Prompt: Sunday drive

Long Shadows Cast by Mars

Jo-Anne Rosen

Billy and I met in a code-crunching sweatshop, "light years ago on another planet," he'd say. When those jobs got outsourced, we were relieved to be unemployed. I liked working with my hands and the way paint smelled when I popped the lid off the can and Billy enjoyed the detail work. I'd get home smelling like turpentine, but I had no missus, so I didn't care. We'd been painting houses together for a couple of years. But his wife had been nagging him to get a better job, so now he was a programmer again and we were wrapping up our business arrangements.

Lucinda served us noodles with canned tuna and melted cheese for dinner, which he assured her was "super yummy comfort food." I said it was "50s retro" and she rolled her eyes and looked away. We didn't get along that well. But I would never let Billy know what I really thought about the missus. He couldn't see she had a mean streak, since almost everything amused him, even or especially Lucinda.

"Hon, look how great Lennie looks in his designer shirt," she needled. "I wish you'd wear something besides those old rags."

"Love me, love my shirts." He laughed and nuzzled her hair.

After we put down a pair of brews with the noodles and some tokes of weed, Billy stood up and flung open the front door. The house was on an unpaved road on the flanks of Sonoma Mountain. "You can just about hear the stars tonight," he announced.

"Shut the door, sweetie," Lucinda said. "It's too drafty."

"A walk'll do us good," he replied cheerily and disappeared into the shadows.

I jumped up to follow and Lucinda huffed along behind, slamming the door.

It was a balmy, cloudless night. Billy was up on the gravel road, head tilted skyward, naming constellations. The moon had not risen but the red planet hung low and brilliant over the top of the hill. It was much more distinct here than in town where I lived.

"Isn't it fantastic?" Billy exclaimed. "We won't see Mars this close ever again."

"It looks the same as last night," Lucinda said.

We walked downhill and our shadows stretched and wobbled faintly yards before us.

"There we go," Billy laughed. "Three long shadows cast by Mars."

Lucinda snorted. "It's the street lights."

"It's poetic license," I said. "Billy, you renewed that license, didn't you?"

"Nah, spaced it out, man. I be operating without a license."

We went on clowning in that vein, while Lucinda fell silent.

Back inside the house Billy re-lit the pipe and opened another bottle. Lucinda insisted that we listen to her favorite CD by "another more famous Lucinda," she said, suddenly husky voiced. These were torch songs with distracting lyrics I'd not heard before, something about love me forever in just three days, or was it three hours. At least she had good taste in music.

In fact, she isn't half bad looking, I was thinking, just as Billy sank back into the easy-rocker, smiled beatifically and nodded off. Lucinda leaned toward me and her breasts plumped up in the low-cut blouse. She had a narrow waist and full hips.

"Lennie, whatever happened to your girlfriend?" she murmured.

"Let's not go there," I said.

"I'm sorry. I didn't realize it was still a sore spot." She clapped one hand over her heart.

"It's a private spot," I cautioned.

"I see." Her eyes were moist and sympathetic.

By then Billy's snores were competing with the music. "Some nights I have to sleep on the couch," Lucinda complained.

Maybe I should have left right then. But she began to clear the dinner table and I felt obliged to help. We were in the brightly-lit kitchen scraping and rinsing plates together, which seemed hilarious to her, I'll never know why. Suddenly anything I said was funny. When she boogied back into the living room I followed as if pulled by invisible threads.

Billy was flat out copping Z's, head lolling to one side, a picture of innocence. Wake up, man, I pleaded silently. No, that's a lie. The truth is that Lucinda now had my full attention.

She danced around the rocker three times then undulated toward me, arms weaving the air, Nothing wrong with dancing, I told myself.

She brushed against me in passing, I took her arm and whirled her close, away, closer. When the beat subsided I took her in my arms for a slow dance, and I heard both Lucindas crooning about oceans of love.

That's when I pulled her tightly to me, and for one long moment she seemed to swell into my embrace. Then she jumped back and hissed, "What are you doing?" Her eyes glittered.

I got out of there as fast as I could. No apology. I bolted. She set me up, I know it. Just like I know for a fact we were drunk and stoned. These are not excuses. I never liked Lucinda much and Billy was the best of friends. She told him something, I know that too. Because he doesn't talk to me anymore unless he has to and when he does he's cordial but cool. And there's nothing I can say to undo that night and put things back the way they were.

I'd feel the same way if he'd come on to my woman. I'd feel betrayed.

And if he were to slap my back over a beer and say, hey old buddy, let's forgive and forget, I might have to tell him, not for a light year, pal, not on this planet.

Previously published in *Flashquake*, Vol. 9, Issue 2, Winter 2010

Prompt: Betrayal

So Small an Outrage

Jo-Anne Rosen

S ally was introduced to Rafael at her neighbor's backyard party. It was a foggy July fourth on Ocean Beach.
Guests huddled around the barbecue coals for warmth.

"You two should meet," her hostess trilled. "You're in the
same field."

Rafael loomed over them, dark and sleek. He had a well-
trimmed beard and mustache, black flecked with silver. He
took her hand, a brief warm pressure.

"A pleasure," he murmured.

"Likewise," Sally said. "So, what's your game?"

He laughed, showing even white teeth. Like a domesti-
cated shark, she thought, and steeled herself. But it was no use.

Rafael worked for a foundation that funded projects in
developing nations. He traveled a great deal and spoke several languages fluently. Sally was a contract fundraiser and
grant writer. She worked at her kitchen table, where heaps
of paper and unanswered phone calls awaited her.

Within minutes they were involved in a heated exchange
of ideas whose subtext she quickly recognized as a volup-
tuous invitation. Firecrackers exploded somewhere, and she
said, "I'd love to see the fireworks for once."

"Let's go." He spread out both arms and hands in a ges-
ture that was to grow familiar. Suddenly they were in his
white MG convertible roaring over the Golden Gate, laughing and excited, watching the dismal fog turn to cream puffs
and the gauzy fireworks explode, eating succulent oysters in
Tiburon under a lush full moon. How easily she had slipped

into his embrace that night, and afterward at every possible opportunity.

She was a plump, pale blonde with a wild sudden laugh and cynical streak, dry as tinder until he touched her. He was tall and slender, a runner, muscled and sun burnished.

Yet he was the first man who matched her appetites, the only man in her acquaintance who ate slowly and with relish. They were both omnivorous readers, curious explorers. On Sunday mornings they read the *New York Times* in bed, then rolled around on it, washed the newsprint off and made love again.

"You're my equal," he told her, and seemed astonished.

She put her toes in his mouth. "Only your equal?"

"I adore uppity women," he murmured.

Their love making was unlike anything she had experienced before, not in its specifics but as a consuming presence in her life. If she couldn't have Rafael in the flesh she dreamed him.

He was often out of town on business. She was often busy and distracted. Two of her children still lived at home, though barely. Her widowed ex-mother-in-law phoned every other day, her crazy ex-husband wanted to reconcile. She either had too much work or not enough. The phone got turned off when she didn't pay the bill on time. Her house grew cluttered and dusty, her clothing held together with safety pins. Rafael said he liked the chaos. What drew him to her was a sense of living on the edge.

They were most often together in his apartment on Potrero Hill. It was quiet and clean with floor to ceiling bookshelves, a spotless kitchen, and a view of the Bay from the bed. No personal photographs, she noted. He had never had children. That he knew about, he said.

Sometimes they went on the road in his MG, up to the mountains or down the coast. Those were the best times, uninterrupted by phone calls. Afterward she would recall, like telling beads, the places where they made love — in rented rooms, in the woods, on a remote beach, even in the little car.

Rafael had a scar on one thigh, a pink puckering of the dark skin, that she liked to lick, because it looked like a little tongue. He shrugged when she asked him how he got it. "Oh that was from a pissed off, ex-girlfriend," he joked. Or was it a joke?

She saw her neighbor approach on the street one day, and then turn abruptly and walk in the opposite direction. It occurred to her that Rafael could have been sleeping with this woman, and then dropped her. It was two weeks since Sally last saw him. He had been on his way to Brasilia.

Perhaps he was seeing another woman?

When next they met for dinner she asked him point blank. He denied it.

But a few months later he took her hand and said, "Sally, I can't lie to you."

He doesn't want me enough anymore to lie, she thought miserably.

That wasn't the end. There might never be an end. Something this intense wasn't going to evaporate, she knew. He would come back to her in between or even during other affairs. She might adjust and take what she could or she might tell him to fuck himself. What was almost unbearable at first was the loss of pure absorption, of being utterly awash in love. She felt stripped to the bone, betrayed. Suddenly she wanted everything she knew she couldn't have.

Late one night she jumped into her car and it shuddered and died. She opened the hood, cursing her bad luck, groping for some part of the engine she knew it helped to thump. The car started. She gunned the motor and took off. In a daze she drove toward Potrero, no clear idea in mind, cruising.

That was Rafael's car alright, parked a mile from his apartment. She pulled into the nearest empty space and got out and stared at the immaculate white body and leather seats, a sour taste in her mouth. You prick, she thought. She looked around the deserted street.

Sally let the air out of one tire. But it wasn't enough. One by one she released the air from the other three. The car soughed and sank and looked forlorn. She imagined his face in the morning, dark with fury. He might guess who had done this. He might even understand how lucky he was to have sustained so small an outrage.

Previously published in *Roman Candles,* 2004

Prompt: Write the last line first

Jo-Anne Rosen

Jo-Anne Rosen, originally from Toronto, has spent most of her time since 1969 in the San Francisco Bay Area. She is a book and website designer, living in Petaluma. She also publishes an online literary journal at www.echapbook.com and is co-editor of the Sonoma County Literary Update (www.socolitupdate.com).

Her fiction has appeared in *Other Voices, The Florida Review, The Summerset Review, Pithead Chapel, Valparaiso Fiction Review, Lime Hawk* and several other journals. *What They Don't Know* is her first fiction collection.

Some of her stories have been performed at Off the Page reader's theater and at the New Short Fiction Series in Hollywood, California.

For more information and links to publications, see: www.joannerosen.us.

Words of Encouragement

The best advice I got from my college "creative writing" professor (Lester Goran) was: If you want to be a writer, write! He went on to say we should write every day or as often as possible. It's like the old joke about how to get to Carnegie Hall: practice, practice, practice.

Unfortunately I did not always follow that advice. And yet, eventually, in the course of a busy and often stressful life, I managed to focus on writing and bit by bit get better at it. So don't beat yourself up for procrastinating; you'll get the writing done if you truly want to. And it's never too late.

The second best advice I got years later from Bob Gluck (who teaches at San Francisco State). He didn't make it up; he passed it on: Kill your darlings.

Yes, I learned to slash and cut, sometimes pages of darlings. For me, revising a story is fun and it's not only about craft. In the process the story often deepens and makes more sense. Here's a link to a wonderful article by George Saunders on that process: www.theguardian.com/books/2017/mar/04/what-writers-really-do-when-they-write

Gloves

Susan Bono

About fifteen years ago, I bought a pair of white Victorian-era, over-the-elbow kidskin gloves at a little junk shop. They are soft and warm as skin always is, whether covering flesh or not. When I take them out of their box, they have a permanent fold above the wrist because they are too long to be stored otherwise. The wrists have four-inch vertical slits on the underside made to be closed with three tiny mother-of-pearl buttons. The shopkeeper described how back in the old days, a young woman's arms had to remain covered at balls and parties, but at suppertime, she could slip her hands out of those slits, tuck the empty fingers out of the way, and eat without soiling the leather.

I don't know if I believed that explanation then, and I strongly doubt it now, but I went ahead and bought those gloves even though they were made for a woman whose dimensions seem impossible—the arms are nearly as long as mine, but the fingers are child-sized, and the wrists are not much thicker than broom handles. That may sound grotesque, but the gloves are so lovely, they'd have to make any wearer look graceful.

I have often considered getting rid of them, but I haven't found the heart yet. Such gloves are part of a dream that began when I was a young girl, a dream of long gowns and carefully placed hair combs and dressing for dinner and men in black tails and ties and the swish of satin slippers on dance floors.

"You have delicate bones," my mother used to say in such a way that I knew she hoped I'd stay fragile. For the longest time, I did my best. I grew up wishing I had porcelain skin, spun gold for hair, and a voice as soft as a dove's. I thought my best shot at Happily Ever After was a Prince Charming who would rescue me from boredom and loneliness.

It took me quite a while to realize such dreams are prisons. The happiest women I know are the ones who rescue themselves and learn to embrace life in all its imperfections. Most days I'm glad to be alive in this messy, often disappointing world, which, despite its faults, offers up more opportunities for magic than can be found in any fairy tale. But I keep these gloves as proof that a woman like the one I dreamed of becoming did exist. When I hold those tiny hands in mine, she dances toward me out of the past, light as a feather, smiling and beautiful, reminding me that anything is possible.

Prompt: Write about finding something at a thrift or antique store

Potato Masher

Susan Bono

I don't even have to be in the kitchen to feel its celluloid handle against my palm, rounded and easy to grab, unlike other potato mashers I've owned. At the other end of this handle waits a circle of stainless steel pierced with small square holes held by two silvery struts in perfect mashing position. I think this tool is technically known as a potato ricer, but no one in my family ever spoke of riced potatoes. No one spoke of the implement to create them, either. But my grandmother's mashed potatoes, always a smooth, white, creamy mass, firm enough to hold a crater for gravy without cracking, were a thing of beauty that could be depended on, and this was what she used to make them. It was in her kitchen from before I was born until I was grown with a house and children of my own. When she was in her nineties and moving to a place where she didn't have to cook, I rescued the masher from the garage sale pile. I couldn't believe my luck. I still can't.

Prompt: I keep it because ...

Prince Charming Five Years Later

Susan Bono

It was a dream come true, the day he found me. Who would have believed he'd beat the odds, scouring the kingdom with that glass slipper in hand, patiently wading through seas of bare feet until he found mine?

But that's the thing about Terrence, he's single-minded and determined. Once he sets his sights on something, there's no stopping him. It took us sixteen months to find a bedroom set for the castle. He had to research every mattress maker in the kingdom, studying all their techniques and test driving the merchandise.

If you think that part sounds like fun, you don't know Terrence. I'm not at liberty to reveal too much, but let's just say he has fixed ideas about how to do everything, from eating to far more intimate operations. It's exhausting, and at the risk of sounding ungrateful, deeply boring.

I left a life of toil and drudgery that was monotonous to the point of insanity. I was talking to the mice and birds by the end there. When I got my chance at the ball, I thought I'd died and gone to heaven. Don't get me wrong, it's a better life by far, as long as I wear the blue gown on Monday so he can make his little joke about how it looks like it's going to be a blue Monday.

Are you starting to get the picture?

Prompt: Prince Charming five years later

Soap

Susan Bono

Because I am my mother's daughter, I hoard soap. You know, the pretty kind given as genteel gifts, ones that rest like warm eggs in your palm and smell like flowers. They come in old-fashioned-looking boxes or tied with a bit of rustic yarn or satin ribbon. I never buy any for myself, because I'm always three to five bars ahead, and milled soap lasts nearly forever. I store my treasure in the cabinet under the sink in the little pink half bath I think of as mine. My mother kept hers in a drawer of the guest room bureau, along with all the tiny soaps and shampoo bottles she collected from hotels.

There were close to a hundred bars of soap in that drawer when I emptied my parents' house. I wept over them as symbols of a Someday that never arrived for my mother. I gave most of them to a women's shelter, but took a few into my own collection. There they lie, scenting my hand towels with their gracious perfume. I still believe I will get around to using them, unlike the ones I own that are shaped like hearts, fancy shoes, and chickens. Novelties like these will never see a soap dish, because as soon as they're subjected to water and human hands, they begin to look like something else entirely. As a child, I was occasionally given soaps in the form of rabbits, cats, and teddy bears, so I know the state of sad deformity such soap is capable of. These days, I try to avoid reminders of loss. New soap is all about the dream of a pristine, orderly Someday, and I cling to that hope, just as my mother did.

Prompt: Write about something you hoard

Talcum Powder

Susan Bono

I finally found the courage to throw away a forty-seven-year-old box of Love's Glossy Lemon Body Powder I got as a birthday present in 1968. I was a thirteen-year-old who believed that patting this slightly sparkly, now-known-to-be-carcinogenic powder on my person would somehow produce the "smooth, silky, delicious" transformation promised on the side of the round cardboard container. That hopeful girl, who wore her mini-dresses above her knobby knees and slept with Scotch tape holding down her bangs, still stands in front of the full-length mirror on her closet door, wishing she could step into the world that stretches beyond her reflection. The slightly green prismatic light lures her closer, but when she places her palm against the glass, she feels only her aloneness.

As I held for the last time that half-full box of lemon-scented talc with its pale yellow puff barely visible under a dome of dusty plastic, I wanted to conjure that girl out of her mirror and give her a little advice. I wouldn't dream of telling her all she was bound to suffer. I wouldn't even warn her that talcum would be considered deadly one day. I would just encourage her to let the powder go in a year or so, to save herself the trouble of dragging it unused from childhood home to dorm room to apartment, through courtship and marriage, from motherhood to middle age to this very moment. I'd tell her the only sparkle a girl ever needs is what she generates herself, even if she wouldn't believe me.

Prompt: I could never get rid of . . .

Susan Bono

Susan Bono has facilitated writers of all skill levels for more than twenty-five years. She edited and published *Tiny Lights: A Journal of Personal Narrative* from 1995 to 2015, and is currently Editor-in-Chief for the *Noyo River Review*. Her essay collection, *What Have We Here: Essays about Keeping House and Finding Home*, was published in 2014. She is inspired by writers who make magic around tables in writing groups like Jumpstart. These days, writing about her stuff helps her let some of it go. www.susanbono.com

Words of Encouragement

You are probably never going to write as well as you hope to, but if you keep at it, you sometimes end up writing better than you expected. Those thrilling moments of surprise and insight are what help writers bear their imperfections, and they don't happen if you don't write. That's why any writing is better than no writing. It's the only way you'll ever discover how good you really are.

Baby Blanket

Marlene Cullen

How do you grieve for someone who is still alive? I wonder about this as I sit in a writing workshop on a warm August morning.

Do you mourn the lost relationship and move on? Do you fondly recall what you loved about that person? Maybe you hope the relationship can be resuscitated.

I'm thinking about these things as I sit in a writing workshop with Pat Schneider at a college in the Berkeley hills. Pat has spread a white chenille bedspread on the floor of the old library where our small group meets. A variety of items are displayed on top of the bedspread. Pat likes to use visual prompts for writing because, she says, the world comes to us through our senses. I understand that. As I look at the items I know what they feel like without touching them. I know what some of them taste like. Pat invites us to explore the objects: Crayons, a stuffed monkey, an eraser, a baseball, a red bra, a garnet bracelet, an old glass bottle, a blue satin cap, a metal chain, a railroad spike and much more.

I don't need to touch any of these things. As soon as I saw the bedspread with fringe around the edges, I knew what I had to write about. I wasn't expecting to write about heartbreak. I didn't choose this subject. It chose me. Head bent, pen poised over my notebook, I swallowed around the lump in my throat and began to write, traveling back fifty years. As I wrote, I blinked away the tears that spilled onto my cheeks.

I was eight when my sister was born with several medical problems. She wore glasses tied around her head at four months. She had her first of many surgeries when she was an infant. She was precious and I loved her with all my heart.

The chenille bedspread with the fringe awakened powerful memories of tucking my precious little sister into her crib and covering her with the most delicate, downy-soft, yellow yarn blanket imaginable.

I thought I had tucked her away. I thought I never wondered about her. And mostly I don't. I no longer think about her on her birthday. I no longer wonder what she's doing on Thanksgiving. She resides in a far-away place in my world. So, why now, why this huge emotional, gut churning feeling that brings tears to my eyes? I think it's because of the power of objects. The power of early childhood imprints. These hidden emotions catch me by surprise. The sight of the fringe on the chenille bedspread catapulted me into the past. It's hard to grieve a death when the person is still alive. I grieve the death of a relationship that was once so meaningful. I would have given my life for my little sister.

My baby sister had monthly doctor visits for check-ups, diagnosis, prognosis, operation updates, and evaluations. Fortunately, March of Dimes paid for all of her operations and medical care. As a single mother with three children, and a full-time job, my mother had her hands full. And my mother had strict rules. She never let me stay home from school, no matter what. I could be dying but off to school I would go. Things changed after my sister was born. My mother took me out of school frequently to help take my sister to her doctor appointments. At the time, I thought my mother needed help with carrying all the baby paraphernalia. Now I wonder if she needed help with the emotional luggage as well.

I adored my baby sister more than words can convey. Summer of 1958 I would put my sister in her baby buggy and cover her with a soft yellow blanket. Taking her for a walk around our block in San Francisco's Mission District, up the alley we'd go, carefully, because there were no sidewalks. Walking past the car mechanics on the corner, their blue jumpsuits and hands grimy with black grease, I quickened my pace because they scared me. Turning the corner, we strolled another block. Past the gas station, we turned the corner. Safe on a sidewalk, I could now really enjoy my baby sister peeking out from her cocoon. Two more blocks and we were back in our alley, our playground, our backyard, home territory, home stretch.

Into our backyard, safe again. Close the gate, latch the metal fastener with a satisfying click. Scoop my sister up from the baby buggy, warm, cuddly, and content in her yellow baby blanket with the fringe around the edges.

Prompt: Visual: Blanket with fringe

Final Score

Marlene Cullen

Julie lifts the faded flower print apron from the hook and puts it on, ready to gather ingredients to make Nana's noodles. Opening the refrigerator door, she gets out two eggs.

As Julie carries the salt and flour to the counter she thinks of the many names of her grandmother: Mabel, her adult name; Phoebe, her childhood nickname; Ma, her kids called her; and Nana; perhaps her favorite name of all.

Mabel wore her apron every day, even to parties. She made all her clothes, always choosing a small flower print design and colorful bias tape for trim around the edges of her aprons. On Tuesdays she made chicken potpie for dinner while listening to her beloved San Francisco Giants on the radio, stirring flour, eggs, salt, and water together.

Mabel scraped the flour mixture from the bowl onto a floured wooden board, concentrating on the baseball game while kneading the dough. McCovey on first, Willie Mays at bat. "Fly ball to center field," Russ Hodges announced. Mabel shaped the mixture into a ball, then pressed down with the palm of her hand. She patiently flattened the dough from one edge to the other with her wood rolling pin. When the dough was thin enough, she shaped it into a long roll.

"McCovey safe on second, Orlando Cepeda at bat," Hodges announced. Mabel used a serrated knife to cut the dough into strips of noodles.

Julie remembers that her grandmother used a large yellow ceramic bowl to mix the dough for noodles. But she doesn't recall what kind of spoon her grandmother used. As Julie turns on the electric mixer to stir the dough, she thinks of her father.

"Maybe he was a genius," she muses. "A genius who couldn't cope with everyday living." Julie turns on the radio to listen to the ball game. As Will Clark comes up to bat, Julie remembers the story about the time her father came running into the house, covered with blood.

As Felipe Alou stepped up to the plate, Mabel thought about the day her oldest son came running into the house, screaming loud enough to wake the dead. He appeared to be covered with blood. Her heart beat so hard she thought it was going to burst. When he started laughing, she looked closer and saw it was catsup. She wanted to box his ears for that prank.

Julie stops the mixer and scrapes the dough onto a floured plastic pastry sheet. Patting the flour mixture into a round shape, she folds it into itself, enjoying the rhythm of kneading. Rolling the dough into a thin sheet with the same wood rolling pin her grandmother used, she listens to the radio absent-mindedly, vaguely aware that Will Clark is on third and Robby Thompson is up at bat. As Julie cuts the dough into strips, she remembers how Nana would give her the job of shaking out the noodles before dropping them into hot chicken broth. If Nana noticed how much dough she ate, she never said anything.

Clark scores as Thompson makes it safe to first. Julie sets the noodles aside, to be added last to the chicken soup she is making.

Mabel put the noodles into the pot with the pieces of chicken, carrots, celery and broth. She rolled out another ball of dough to cover the top of the chicken potpie. Sliding the pot into the oven, she looked at the clock and saw it was forty-five minutes until the table needed to be set for dinner. She might as well do some ironing.

Reaching for the red blouse at the top of the ironing basket. Mabel thought about Julie as she ironed the collar of her grand-daughter's blouse.

"I hope she knows her father loves her in his own way." She ironed the sleeves and then the front of the blouse. "I know she won't visit him in the hospital. Might be too late anyway." Pressing the iron along the back of the blouse, Mabel thought about how Julie didn't really know her father. Mabel pondered how to tell Julie a few stories about her father and how much alike they were.

Julie gathers four blouses that need to be ironed. She pulls out the small ironing board from the drawer in the laundry room.

"What would Nana think about an ironing board in a drawer?" Julie wonders, ironing the blouse the way Nana taught her. First the collar, then the sleeves. Flatten one front side on the ironing board, then the other side and last, the back. Finishing the blouses, Julie wonders what else she can iron. Walking to the couch where a pile of laundry waits to be folded she picks out her daughter's pale green sheets. Julie likes the sound of the baseball game in the background even though she isn't paying much attention. It reminds her of her grandmother.

After dinner dishes were washed, dried, and put away, Mabel picked up her purse and counted out the change she would need for bus fare. Depositing fifteen cents into her pocket, she glanced at her granddaughter, who was hunched over her homework at the kitchen table, struggling with an algebra problem.

"I'll be back around eleven," Mabel said, heading out into the summer night.

The phone rang at 6:15 the next morning. Julie rushed to answer it, angry at whoever was calling so early. Julie didn't want the ringing to wake her grandmother, who had gotten home late from the hospital. The man's voice asked for Mabel.

"She's sleeping and I'm not going to wake her. Who is this?"

"Dr. Holt from San Francisco General. Her son John passed away this morning."

Remembering the phone call as if it were yesterday, Julie still can't believe the doctor would say someone died without knowing who he was talking to. It was as if she didn't exist.

Ironing a scarf, Julie recalls coming home from school one gray day in September. She remembers walking in the front door, going into her bedroom, and setting her jacket and school books on her pink chenille bedspread. She went into the kitchen to fix her Afterschool Snack. That's what she and her grandmother called it, as if Afterschool Snack was a secret recipe they shared. Julie heard the ballgame on the radio. Things seemed to happen in slow motion after that. Julie remembers seeing her grandmother on the porch floor. The iron was still plugged in. Julie's favorite red blouse lay on the ironing board, half-ironed. And the radio announcer saying, "That's a game, folks. Final score, Giants nine, Dodgers three."

Julie leans against the counter and wipes her tears with her faded flower print apron.

Prompt: Apron

Guy Noir, *with a nod to Garrison Keillor*

Marlene Cullen

It was a usual Tuesday afternoon, hot as Hades in the third floor walk-up. But the rent was cheap and the place was private. The trash can overflowed with the remains of bitter coffee in paper cups and the ashtray overflowed with paper clips. I like to make paperchain necklaces. Not a manly thing to do, but keeping my hands busy relaxes my mind. And I need a relaxed mind to be receptive to clues. I haven't made many necklaces lately.

My size tens were propped on my desk, my hat covered my face, blocking out the midday Tampa sun. I was about to doze off when rapping on the glass door startled me.

"Come in, door's unlocked." I took my feet off the desk and placed them on the floor, business like. Then I remembered I forgot to remove the gum on my shoe.

I eyeballed the door as it swung open. In walked a cool breath of fresh air. I tried not to stare. I failed.

"Mr. Noir," the cool breath purred. She hesitated, then extended her right hand. "Miss Scarlett," she smiled.

We shook hands. "Pleased to meet you, Miss Scarlett. What can I do for you? How can I help you?" She might have noticed my shoe was stuck to the floor, but she didn't say anything.

"It's my ..." She opened her pocketbook and took out a dainty white hanky, violet flowers embroidered in each corner. She dabbed at her baby blue eyes.

Real tears, I wondered, or crocodile?

"It's my husband, Mr. Noir. The very wealthy and respectable Mr. Big."

Alarms sounded in my head. Mr. Big. The big shot who owned all of Park Place and Boardwalk.

"What about him?" I inquired.

"He's missing. He's been gone since Thursday."

I quickly calculated. Thursday, Friday, Saturday, Sunday, Monday and now today, Tuesday.

"So, he's been gone … uh …" I counted, finger by finger. Thursday pointer finger, Friday middle finger, Saturday ring finger …

"Five days, Mr. Noir," Miss Scarlett interrupted, "and five long nights."

"Yeah, I see," I said. I was stuck with holding up three fingers. I flattened my hand and smoothed out my hair. "Where did you last see him … uh, Miss Scarlett? And why are you called Miss Scarlett if you are married to Mr. Big?"

"Wednesday night. We went to bed around 11 pm and when I woke up, poof, he was gone."

I noticed she didn't answer my question about her name.

"Anything missing?" I asked, "Clothes, shoes, his wallet?"

"That's just the thing," she sniffed, holding her dainty hanky to her nose. "Nothing is missing. It's as if he just vanished into thin air."

"Have you gone to the police?"

"Really, Mr. Noir, do you think I need that kind of attention?"

"Why did you wait so long to contact me?"

"I kept thinking he'd come back."

"You two have a fight, Miss Scarlett? And why am I calling you Miss Scarlett when you are a married woman?"

"We never quarreled, Mr. Noir."

Again, I noticed she didn't answer my question about her name. Something about her name was familiar.

"That's not what I read in the funny papers, Miss Scarlett."

"Seriously, Mr. Noir, you read that trash?"

"Yeah, it helps me get to sleep at night. Listen, I'll need a retainer of $5,000."

She handed me a thick envelope. I took a look inside and whistled.

"That's a lot of cash to be carrying around."

"I'm not worried."

"How can I reach you?"

"I'll be lounging in the conservatory."

I watched as she sashayed out of the room.

I leaned back in my chair. I had seen all her movies. And the last one, *How To Get Away With Murder*, was about a starlet marrying an older guy. He disappears under mysterious circumstances and she takes a trip to Cancun. My usual sharp-as-a-tack memory cannot recall the ending of this flick. I do remember it wasn't a great movie, but with her looks, who cares about the plot.

Miss Scarlett, I mused, as I picked bits of gum off my shoe. It's a funny thing about dames like her. They marry for the dough, forgetting they have to live with the guy.

Yesterday's society headlines caught my eye. Seems Miss Scarlett recently returned from a trip to Cancun. And it seems she's in line to receive a bucket load of money if her husband's death can be proved. They'll need the body for that. Guess that's where I enter the scene.

I noticed a slip of paper on the floor. It must have fallen out of her pocketbook when she pulled out her handkerchief. It was a receipt for a candlestick.

I could feel the lightbulb shimmering over my head.

Miss Scarlett, in the passageway between the lounge and the conservatory, with a candlestick.

Prompt: Prairie Home Companion CD

Lost

Marlene Cullen

In a foreign country
People standing, walking, talking
Walk through a homeless camp
Cool green water in canal
People standing, walking, talking
Floating in a pool of clear blue water
Cool green water in canal
Exposed
Floating in a pool of clear blue water
Walk through a homeless camp
Exposed
In a foreign country
Confused
Lost in a foreign city
Red Tour bus
Lady with ginger hair
Lost in a foreign city
Smiled gently
Lady with ginger hair
Surprised in my own bed
Smiled gently
Red Tour bus
Surprised in my own bed
Confused

Prompt: Write a pantoum.

Summer 1974

Marlene Cullen

Still in the bliss of being a newlywed, I signed on to be part of a five-member crew on the 60-foot schooner, *Gold Star*, sailing from San Francisco to Hawaii. I wasn't worried about being the only female aboard. I had spent many Sundays sailing with my husband, Jim, father-in-law, Larry, and friends around San Francisco Bay.

We expected it would take us twenty days to sail from San Francisco to Hilo. I didn't expect to jump ship.

We left the harbor mid-morning on a sultry June day in 1974. Once past the breakwater, we raised the sails and glided under the Golden Gate Bridge. As soon as we were on the open ocean, choppy seas lifted us up the crests of the waves and down into the troughs, causing all of us to be seasick, except Captain Larry. As we barreled along in heavy winds, I thought, "We'll make it to tropical paradise in record time." I looked forward to lounging on white sands, lazing in the sun, and terra firma under my feet.

After eight years of sailing on the *Gold Star*, I felt confident and competent as a crew member. I also had complete confidence in my crew mates, especially my father-in-law's ability to navigate. I usually felt relaxed at the helm, but our first evening at sea, I had to grip the wheel with both hands to keep us on a steady course. Even though I wore foul weather gear, everything I had on was soaked. Jim took his turn at the wheel at the end of my one-hour watch. I gratefully headed into the warm and dry galley.

After a few minutes, Jim discovered that instead of feeling

pressure when he tried to turn the wheel, it easily spun around. Too easily. It turned out, the steering gear was no longer attached to the rudder. We were 100 miles off the coast, headed due west towards open seas with no way to control our steering. Jim and Larry quickly removed the wheel housing to see if they could repair the steering gear.

Fortunately, Larry had just taken a sun shot with the sextant, our only form of navigation. While Larry, Jim, and Jesse took the steering gear apart, Steve and I began the math calculations to determine our location. When we finished the computations, Larry called the Monterey Coast Guard on the VHF band radio. The 95-foot cutter *Cape Wash* was on the way to rescue us.

There was nothing more for me to do, so I climbed into my bunk. Even with rough seas, howling winds, and our perilous situation, I felt secure and safe, comfortably wedged into my bunk. The *Gold Star* was a solid and well-built vessel. I was confident about her seaworthiness.

At 4 a.m., the winds lightened enough for us to go on deck to haul the booms around and maneuver the sails, changing our direction from open-ocean towards land. We had to be hooked up to our lifelines the entire time we were on deck, or we would have been swept overboard by the violent waves. For half a day, we just hung on. Heavy winds prevented us from going on deck, no one had an appetite so we didn't prepare food. The *Gold Star* propelled herself towards our rescue boat. I hung on and hoped we would soon be rescued.

It took the *Cape Wash* crew twelve hours to reach us. We cheered when we spotted the Coast Guard vessel through the thick fog, but our troubles weren't over yet. It was challenging to get the Coast Guard vessel close enough to throw us a line. Maneuvering in heavy seas, the *Cape Wash* got too close, causing damage to our hull, tore out some rigging, and ripped a sail. Finally, a tow rope was thrown which Jim caught and belayed around a cleat. The tow back was a like being on a rollercoaster under a waterfall, for twelve hours.

At the entrance to Monterey harbor, a smaller Coast Guard boat guided us through the narrow entrance, around other boats and into a berth. After the stomach-churning ride through choppy waters, I climbed out of the boat on wobbly legs, thankful to be on land.

Jim, Larry, and Jesse replaced the steering gear. Steve and I hung our wet clothes and sleeping bags out to dry. We repaired the hull, replaced the rigging, and stitched the sails.

Four days later, we continued our ocean crossing to Hawaii.

For much of the trip, the routine was reading, chatting, repairing sails, and learning how to tie nautical knots. Deciding what to wear was easy. If it was hot, wear shorts and a light-weight top. If it was cold, put on a jacket. We were able to play cards until one of the crew members got tired of losing at cribbage and threw the deck of cards into the sea. It was the only deck on board. This same crew member got fed up with the lack of punctuation in the e.e. cummings book he was reading and flung it overboard.

Cooking onboard required careful planning. To save on fuel, we cooked multiple things at once. We baked bread in the oven while cooking dinner and heating water on the stove top. The angle of the tilted boat was a consideration. I forgot about that one evening when I decided to make brownies. I mixed the ingredients and poured them into the baking pan. I slid the pan into the oven where it promptly tilted sideways, spilling half the mixture into the oven. I propped up the low side of the pan. When I looked in the oven a while later, I saw the prop I used was too tall and caused the mixture to spill out the other side. The brownies eventually cooked and were delicious. I scraped the hardened mixture off the sides and bottom of the oven and we devoured every bit of it.

Food choices were simple. When we ran out of fresh produce, we had canned meat and canned fruit. We caught a mahi-mahi that was delicious. We took turns cooking and cleaning. When it was my turn to make dinner, I did my best. As a newlywed, I was still learning to cook and wasn't at all confident about my cooking on a rolling and rocking vessel. One night I prepared what I thought was a passable dinner. I was crushed when my father-in-law angrily thrust his plate back at me, reproaching me for how awful it tasted. I retreated to the galley to clean up. His lack of appreciation and critical nature began taking a toll on me.

We were entertained by observing water creatures, both small and large. Leaning overboard we watched tiny Velella jellyfish floating in the water, looking like miniature sailboats. One evening when it was my turn to clean the galley after dinner, I couldn't tear myself away from watching a whale about 300 feet from us. I held vigil on deck, feeling if I could keep it in sight, it wouldn't come too close and possibly capsize us. Perhaps my imagination was working overtime from lack of sleep. That same cards-and-book-tossing crew member kindly cleaned the galley for me. I was so appreciative, I forgave him for his tendency to throw things overboard.

Our schedule was one person at the helm for an hour and four hours off. I especially liked being at the wheel in the middle of the night thinking about family, friends, and experiences. I could dream, plan, and sing. I was surprised by how many songs I didn't know the words to. My dear husband surprised me many times and took my shift, giving me an extra hour's attempt to sleep.

On clear nights stars looked like Tiffany diamonds nestled on a black velvet evening gown. My 5 a.m. turn began in a completely dark cockpit. It felt like a miracle every morning to go from dark to light. No matter if there was any trouble the night before, no matter what fears, insecurities or worries I had, sunrise always cheered me.

Even though I got along with this crew fabulously on weekend sails on San Francisco Bay, my frustrations began to build on this long-distance sail. Captain Larry had strict rules. Each person could only use a quart of water a day. No using the stove just to heat water. We couldn't open the refrigerator door because it let warm air in and drained the battery. On day thirteen, Captain Larry decided we could manage without the refrigerator so he disconnected it. We moved the perishable items into a dishpan with a wet cloth over it, keeping it cool in the cockpit storage area.

While the guys got along seamlessly, I often felt excluded. When my suggestions were ignored, I wondered if I was invisible. I became increasingly discouraged with being misunderstood and tired of being disrespected. I woke up one morning, wondering, "What am I doing here?"

For most of the voyage we were on the same course for several days with the boat tilting at the same angle. But when the wind changed direction and blew from behind the boat, we constantly rolled and rocked from side-to-side. Jars in the refrigerator rattled against one another. Pots and pans made a raucous noise as they slid from side to side. Sails and booms shuddered back and forth, planks creaked. It was tolerable in the daytime, but at night, the cacophony of noise and man-made snoring made sleep impossible for me. I prayed I could hold on until we got to Hilo.

Finally, twenty-one days after we left Monterey Harbor, land was sighted. Hilo was lush with green hills. The water was sparkling blue. We were tired, hungry, and ready for someone else's cooking.

We sailed around the islands, anchoring in coves, and rowing ashore in the dinghy. We enjoyed hiking the emerald green hills, splurging on restaurant food, and walking along beaches. Because of the disconnected refrigerator, we had to row ashore daily to purchase blocks of ice as well as groceries, hauling goods from store to dinghy to the boat.

My most memorable experience was in Kawaihae, at a place that felt like time forgot. Alfie's featured mouth-watering Chicago-style pizza, an extensive variety of beer, and a cast of characters parading in and out.

We sat around a table with six Hawaiians who were making joyful sounds with guitars, ukuleles, and spoons. "Come on, join in," they said, bursting into song. They sang in English, in Spanish, and in Hawaiian. They sang Hava Nagila and selections from Carmen. They sang loud and clear. They bought us a round of beer. The owner bought us a round of beer. We bought a round of beer.

Four hours later, when we reluctantly got up to leave, they serenaded us, their Haole (white) friends, "God bless you, my friend, you'll never meet a Kanocka (Hawaiian) as nice as me." Their friendliness and love for life deeply touched me.

I woke up the next morning, feeling something was terribly wrong, something was missing. My thoughts ping-ponged all morning. Thinking about the lively friends at Alfie's cantina, I realized I was missing camaraderie.

I decided not to sail back to San Francisco. I felt horrible about leaving the *Gold Star* one crew member short, but I couldn't face any more days at sea with these fellows, whom I adored on land and loathed on water.

Jim saw me off at the airport. It was a tearful farewell, but I was giddy with the idea of being on my own.

Returning to our house in San Francisco lifted my spirits. I created, crafted, and painted. Learning how to use a hammer, a drill, and a glue gun, I completed home improvements.

I got together with friends for dinner and movies.

Becalmed with no wind, it took thirty-five days for Jim and the crew to sail back to San Francisco. By the time we reunited, I was rejuvenated, calm, and confident. Jim was enthusiastic to meet the new me.

My summer vacation, my real summer vacation, gave me the gift of myself, even though it meant jumping ship.

Prompt: Write about your summer vacation. Not the "My Summer Vacation" essay you wrote in school in September. Write about what really happened.

Marlene Cullen

Marlene's short stories and essays have been published in literary journals, anthologies, and newspapers, including *Tiny Lights: A Journal of Personal Narrative, Building Bridges, More Bridges, Vintage Voices: A Toast To Life, Vintage Voices: Four-Part Harmony,* and *Vintage Voices: Cent'Anni: May you live 100 years.* She is a member of the California Writer's Club.

Fulfilling her passion for writing and sharing the joy of writing with others, Marlene leads unique workshops where participants often experience transformational changes.

"Marlene has the remarkable capacity to provide two elements essential to every writer: a safe place to write and inspiration. She thinks clearly and listens carefully. I value her responses to my writing."

— A workshop participant

Words of Encouragement

Tell your story. Write what you want to write without worries about how it will turn out.

Write fiction, memoir, non-fiction, poetry, songs, plays, creative non-fiction. Just write!

Producing this book has been a dream of mine for 12 years. I kept writing, learning and refining my writing and editing skills.

Keep dreaming. Keep writing. Work towards accomplishing your dream. Stick to it and someday, your dream will come true, like mine did.

Writing Resources

Freewrites and Writing Prompts

A "freewrite" is "free association" for a quick style of writing. It's a way of writing freely with no worries about the end product.

Any word, a poem, or a phrase will work as a prompt. You can use visual prompts to inspire writing such as objects, photos, artwork, book covers, first line in books, last line in books.

Freewrites are meant to be spontaneous writing. Write thoughts as quickly as they form. These "first thoughts" tap into your creative energy. First thoughts are the way the mind flashes on something. Write quickly so you don't lose the thoughts that are propelling your pen.

Writing in this style is for your personal enjoyment or to enhance your writing. Do not expect "perfect" writing.

Leave your inner critic outside the door. Shrug off the editor that sits on your shoulder. Write whatever comes into your mind.

You can use paper and a pen, a computer, or tablet to write. You can also use paper and a pencil. Experiment to find what method is best for you.

If you get stuck

If you can't think what to write next, write the prompt, literally, write the prompt.

Or, write:

What I really want to say ... Continue writing.

I remember … and go from there.

The trouble started when …

The problem is …

You can use these as your emergency prompts. You can also use the opposite:

I don't want to write about …

I don't remember …

Trust the process. Your mind will give you something to write about.

Rules

As Natalie Goldberg says in *Writing Down the Bones*, there are six rules of writing:

1. Keep the hand moving
2. Don't cross out.
3. Don't worry about spelling, punctuation, or grammar.
4. Lose control.
5. Don't think.
6. Go for the jugular.

Write what you want

Write what you want to write. Don't worry if it's correct, polite, or appropriate.

Keep your hand moving, even if you think you have nothing

to say. Trust yourself. This is the place to feel free to write whatever you want. That's why it's called a freewrite.

Write from your own experience, write about what happened to someone else, or respond to the prompt as your fictional character would respond. Don't have a fictional character? Maybe this is the time to create a character.

Prompts

If you use prompts that draw from your childhood, you will have endless material to write about.

As Brenda Ueland says in *If You Want to Write*, "Tell about some childhood memory, write it as carelessly, recklessly, fast and sloppily as possible. Forget about writing 'writing,' and about trying to please the teacher. Tell what you remember spontaneously, impulsively.

"Write about your childhood experiences. A child experiences things from his or her true self (creatively) and not from his or her theoretical self (dutifully), i.e., the self he thinks he ought to be. That is why childhood memories are the most living and sparkling and true."

You can also use these freewrites for writing fiction. Perhaps you're having a hard time making your character seem real. You can use an experience from your own childhood and write as if your character sled down the hill, broke her nose, and fell in love with a stranger.

Going for the jugular gives you permission to write the truth, not the sugar coated version you write in Christmas letters. Tell the truth. You always thought Uncle Ed was creepy. You don't like kale. You love the smell of freshly cut grass.

Telling the truth allows you to write on a deep, meaningful level, and eliminate the fluff.

Ready to write?

Choose a prompt from *Discoveries*. Set a timer for 15-20 minutes. Begin writing, using the prompt as an inspirational start to your writing.

For additional prompts please go to The Write Spot Blog: www.TheWriteSpot.us

"Writing isn't about the destination — writing is the journey that transforms the soul and gives meaning to all else."

— Sue Grafton

Writing Groups

Whether you want to write poetry, fiction, non-fiction, flash fiction, or memoir, or if you are experiencing writer's block, a freewrite-style writing group may be the answer to accomplishing your writing desires.

The freewrite style of writing, using prompts, can be thought of as writing practice, just as badminton players practice to improve their skills, writers write to improve their writing skills.

Getting Started

Ask friends, invite fellow attendees at literary events, go on social media to find like-minded writers to join you in this adventure.

Meet in a coffee shop, library, bookstore, community center, senior center, a park in nice weather, or someone's home to write.

Meet weekly, twice a month, or monthly.

Using Prompts

Use a variety of prompts. Write for 15-20 minutes on each prompt.

When it's Time to Stop Writing

When it's time to stop writing on each prompt, you can ring a bell, tap on a bowl, or simply say, "Two minutes to stop writing." Or, as I like to say at the end of each writing time, "Finish your thought, finish your sentence, come to a good stopping place."

Read Aloud

Depending on the size of the group and how much time is allotted, read one or more freewrites out loud. Most people are nervous about this. To overcome that, think of yourself as a machine, transcribing the written word to oral. After a while, it will be apparent that reading out loud enriches the writing experience. Plus, you get to hear a variety of responses to the same prompt.

Reflective Feedback

Participants are invited to comment on what they especially like, what they remember, or what stands out about the writing. This is not the time for critiquing nor judging. This writing is not to be dissected nor analyzed.

Ready?

Start right now, as practice for your writing group. Get some paper and a fast moving pen. Glance at your clock, note the time. Write for ten minutes about "trees." After that, write for ten minutes, using "I remember" as your prompt. Next, go with, "What I really want to say."

How to Write a Pantoum

The Pantoum is a poem made up of stanzas whose four lines are repeated in a pattern: Lines 2 and 4 of each stanza are repeated as lines 1 and 3 of the next stanza. The final stanza has a twist: The second and fourth lines are the same as the third and first lines of the first stanza. The first line of the poem is the same as the last. This way, every line is used twice.

Stanza 1:

_____ line 1

_____ line 2

_____ line 3

_____ line 4

Stanza 2:

_____ line 5
same as line 2

_____ line 6

_____ line 7
same as line 4

_____ line 8

Stanza 3:

_____ line 9
same as line 6

_____ line 10
same as line 3

_____ line 11
same as line 8

_____ line 12
same as line 1

Narrative Technique — Intercutting

Weave two stories together, one happening in present tense, one happened in past tense.

Intercutting is similar to flashback: Open the story in a particular time, then move backwards in time, revealing scenes that led up to current time in the story line.

How to intercut:

Write a scene in present tense in which a character is engaged in an activity while thinking about an event that happened in the past. This can be written in third person point of view (he, she, it) or first person point of view (I).

Write a second scene, this time in past tense, either with a new character, or the same character in the previous scene. Use the same idea: character is engaged in an activity while thinking about an event that happened in the past.

Weave the two scenes together, going back and forth between scenes.

Add details.

See "Final Score" by Marlene Cullen for an example of intercutting.

Recommended Books on Writing

Books on writing are gems in our treasure chest of writing resources. Here are some of my favorites.

Aronie, Nancy Slonim — *Writing From the Heart*
Baldwin, Christina — *Storycatcher*
Barrington, Judith — *Writing the Memoir, From Truth to Art*
Baty, Chris — *No Plot? No Problem!*
Bennet, Hal Zina — *Write From The Heart*
Brande, Dorothea — *Becoming a Writer*
Cameron, Julia — *The Artist's Way*
         — *The Right to Write*
Clegg, Eileen M. — *Claiming Your Creative Self*
DeSalvo, Louis — *Writing As A Way of Healing*
Epel, Naomi — *Writers Dreaming*
George, Elizabeth — *Write Away*
Goldberg, Natalie — *Wild Mind*
         — *Writing Down the Bones*
Keene, Sam and Anne Valley-Fox — *Your Mythic Journey*
Kelton, Nancy Davidoff — *Writing From Personal Experience*
King, Stephen — *On Writing*
Lauber, Lynn — *Listen to Me*
Lamott, Anne — *Bird by Bird*
Lara, Adair — *Naked, Drunk, and Writing*
Le Guin, Ursula K. — *Steering the Craft*
Rosenfeld Jordan — *Make a Scene*
Saltzman, Joel — *If You Can Talk, You Can Write*
Schneider, Pat — *Writing Alone And With Others*
Smith, Michael C. and Suzanne Greenberg — *Everyday Creative Writing*
Sternburg, Janet — *The Writer on Her Work*
Ueland, Brenda — *If You Want to Write*

Acknowledgements

Thank you to my co-writers and writing teachers for extraordinary experiences. I'm grateful we shared space in a classroom, around a table, on chairs and couches, creating opportunities for expansive writing.

A huge bouquet of appreciation to all the writers I have had the pleasure of writing with: Wild Mindz, Jumpstart, and others. Thank you for your trust in the process, your confidence in one another, and for your faith in me.

When I listen to writing that was just created in Jumpstart, I'm in awe. It's as if, on the way to Jumpstart, writers swallowed a magic pill, opening a portal to exceptional writing.

Serendipity led me to Susan Bono. On that first day we met in her cozy writing space, I had no idea how deep our friendship would become. Thanks for all your hand-holding, your advice, your wisdom, and thanks for being my comrade on this writing-life journey.

I tip my hat to Jo-Anne Rosen, book designer and formatter extraordinaire. Your patience, attention to detail, your "catches," your knowledge amaze me. I could not have accomplished this book without you.

Thank you to all the Writers Sampler and Writers Forum presenters, too many to list individually, for sharing your knowledge and wisdom about the craft and business of writing.

My first inspirational writing teacher was Lee Bacon, 1978, Petaluma, California, who offered creative writing prompts and constructive comments.

A special thanks to teachers who taught a variety of writing techniques and were instrumental in smoothing the rough edges of my writing to polished pieces, often leading to publication (next page).

- Adair Lara — Her workshops and classes in her home were informative, delightful, entertaining, and fun!
- Christine Walker — A gifted teacher who created the mini-MFA program.
- Clara Rosemarda — Her remarkable intuition and ability to engage deep writing is very much appreciated.
- Frances Lefkowitz — Her honest writing is a primer for how to write memoir.
- Guy Biederman — Guides writers from freewrites to finished work in an easy, you-can-do-this style.
- Jordan Rosenfeld — An expert in writing scene and creating memorable writing prompts.
- Natalie Goldberg — An amazing weekend in Tiburon, including an insightful slow walk.
- Pat Schneider — Heartfelt in her passion to help writers develop writing.
- Susan Bono — Writes the most amazing freewrites, facilitates instructive writing groups, and shepherds writers to completion of novels.
- Susan Hagen — Gathers writers and gives them the gift of meaningful writing.
- Terry Ehret — A gifted poet who introduced the pantoum and intercutting to me and I'm forever grateful.
- Victoria Zackheim — A patient, thoughtful, and thorough writing teacher.

> A deep breath, a big sigh, and a hearty hug to my writing buddy and dear friend, Pat Tyler. You will live in my heart forever.

About Marlene

My enthusiasm for writing began when I was four years old, scribbling large loops across big sheets of paper, pretending to write. When I was nine, I jotted notes in a little spiral-bound notebook, recording the activities of family members, journalistic style. Now I scribble in larger notebooks, spiral-bound still my favorite choice. I love discovering fictional characters as they unfurl from my imagination.

In 2002, I invited a few friends to write twice a month with me in my parlor. Two years later, I began facilitating Jumpstart Writing Workshops. Wanting to bring writing information to a larger group, I launched The Write Spot Blog, a place to share information about writing: Places to submit, writing prompts, inspiration, quotes, recommended books, editors, writing websites, and more.

There are over 300 writing prompts on The Write Spot Blog, plenty to choose from. www.TheWriteSpot.us

I have been published in several anthologies, won some contests and honorable mentions. I can research for hours, discovering information about writing, writers, and publishing. I delight in sharing my findings with you on The Write Spot Blog.

The idea for this book was conceived in 2005. It took twelve years to make it happen. A very long gestation period, but an important period of time to learn, absorb, tweak my original idea and here we are, a finished product. At last.

My personal life has grown much like my writing life, steady with some bumps along the way, and always moving in a positive direction.

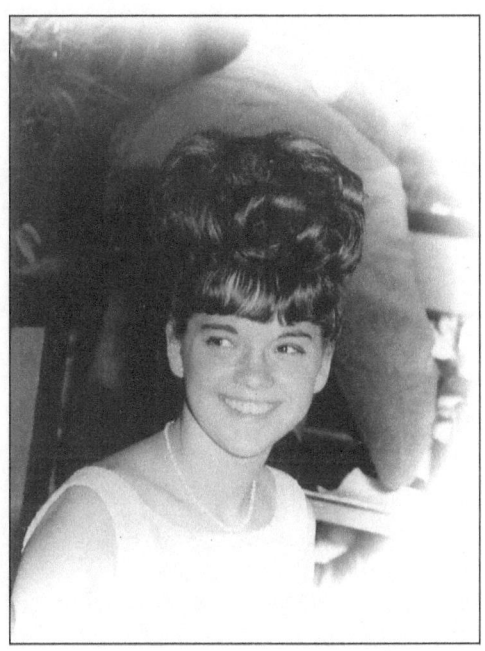

Marlene at the Tonga Room,
Fairmont Hotel, San Francisco. June 1965

In the summer of 1966 I took a chance and went on a blind date. On a sunny Saturday, my date and I went to the Santa Cruz Boardwalk, returned to San Francisco and enjoyed dinner at Tad's Steak house on Powell Street. Jim and I married in 1969. We live in rural Northern California where our three children grew up and our granddaughters visit Camp Cullen.

www.ingramcontent.com/pod-product-compliance
Lightning Source LLC
Chambersburg PA
CBHW022155260626
47155CB00018B/2052